W9-BIV-879

DATE DUE

DEMCO 38-296

CLONING

Other books in the At Issue series:

CLONING

Bruno Leone, *Book Editor*

Daniel Leone, *President*
Bonnie Szumski, *Publisher*
Scott Barbour, *Managing Editor*
Helen Cothran, *Series Editor*

GREENHAVEN
PRESS ®

™

GALE

San Diego • Detroit • New York • San Francisco • Cleveland
New Haven, Conn. • Waterville, Maine • London • Munich

LIBRARY OF CONGRESS CATALOGING-IN-PUBLICATION DATA

Cloning / Bruno Leone, book editor.
    p. cm. — (At issue)
    Includes bibliographical references and index.
    ISBN 0-7377-1339-9 (pbk. : alk. paper) — ISBN 0-7377-1338-0 (lib. : alk. paper)
        1. Cloning—Social aspects. 2. Human cloning—Social aspects. 3. Cloning—Moral and ethical aspects. 4. Cloning—Religious aspects. I. Leone, Bruno, 1939– . II. At issue (San Diego, Calif.)
    QH442.2 .C5642 2003
    174'.966—dc21
                                                                    2002074278

Printed in the United States of America

Contents

Page

Introduction

In 1964 John Gurdon, an Oxford University biologist and researcher, asexually reproduced a species of amphibian called an African claw frog. By implanting the nucleus taken from one frog's intestinal cells into the enucleated egg of a female frog, Gurdon succeeded in producing a clone, an exact biological replica of the donor frog. While many scientists responded with praise and enthusiasm for Gurdon's achievement, it received very little attention in the worldwide media. Apparently, the cloning of a frog was not considered particularly newsworthy.

However, when Ian Wilmut, an embryologist working with a team of scientists at the Roslin Institute in Edinburgh, Scotland, successfully cloned a female sheep in 1996, the media reacted by publishing countless stories on Wilmut's experiment and airing numerous interviews featuring experts debating the pros and cons of cloning. Unlike Gurdon's amphibian frog, the sheep, named Dolly, was a member of a taxonomic class of animals called *mammalia*. Moreover, it seemed to escape no one's attention that the most prominent species belonging to the class *mammalia* are humans.

Judging from the reaction to Dolly, it was obvious that Wilmut and his associates had carried cloning into forbidden territory. The overwhelming response to his pioneering effort from governments and private groups throughout the world was clamorously negative. Interestingly enough, the criticism was not directed at the embryologist and his researchers for cloning a sheep, but rather at what was assumed to be the logical next step in the cloning saga, namely, attempts to clone a human being. The National Bioethics Advisory Commission, established in 1995 to counsel the president of the United States on bioethical questions, issued a report in 1997 advising against government support of American scientists engaged in human cloning. Heeding its advice and backed by the Clinton administration, several members of Congress immediately introduced legislation to ban human cloning. With a rare show of support for his predecessor's policy, President George W. Bush declared his complete opposition to any form of human cloning while several members of Congress during the Bush administration have referred to those contemplating human cloning as "mad scientists" engaged in "ghoulish work." Other nations have followed suit, including the Islamic Republic of Iran, whose ruling council has decreed the death penalty for any scientist engaged in human cloning. Ironically, for over two thousand years prior to the cloning of Dolly, humans were successfully cloning plants by using grafts and stem cuttings. Clearly it was the cloning of a mammal that gave rise to the world's concern. Some of this anxiety, of course, stems from the belief that human cloning is just around the corner, but, the fact is, cloning any organism is still a difficult and complicated process.

Cloning is a form of asexual reproduction in which the offspring or clone is a carbon copy of the donor organism. For example, if a human were successfully cloned, the offspring would possess all of the physical characteristics of the donor parent including hair and eye color, voice, skin pigmentation, birthmarks, and fingerprints. Moreover, the clone would even inherit whatever talents and abilities (musical, intellectual, athletic) the parent possessed provided that those abilities derive from the parent's genetic makeup.

Cloning is a deceptively simple procedure and is based upon the fact that every cell in every living organism (with the exception of sex cells) contains a precise genetic duplicate of the organism itself. A donor contributes the nucleus from any one of his or her body cells. The nucleus is then injected into an enucleated egg taken from a female of the same species as the donor. Once the transfer has occurred, an electrical charge or other stimulus is applied to the egg, tricking it into dividing as though a sperm had fertilized it in the natural way. Once the resulting embryo has reached a stage of fetal development known as a blastocyst (four to five days after fertilization), it is then transferred into the uterus of a surrogate mother.

As simple as cloning may appear in theory, in practice, however, it presents numerous and difficult obstacles. For example, the female's egg must be selected and nucleated at a critical moment in its maturity. Several hours too soon or too late will result in a failure to fertilize. Also, removing the nucleus from the donor cell is an excruciatingly delicate matter. Any alteration of the chromosomal structure of the nucleus during the removal process will result in genetic damage and a failure to fertilize. (It is a fact that during the procedure involving nuclear removal, genetic damage occurs far more often than not.) And equally important, the nucleus must be extracted at a certain stage of cellular development in order to be viable. The team of scientists responsible for the birth of Dolly experienced two hundred and seventy-seven frustrating failures before finally succeeding.

Unquestionably, opponents of cloning greatly outnumber supporters of the procedure. While some advocacy groups such as the American Anti-Vivisection Society argue that animal cloning is cruel, the overwhelming majority of opposition is directed not at animal cloning but at the future possibility of widespread reproductive human cloning. Critics of human cloning fall into several categories including, among others, religious, ethical, moral, and sociological. There are those who view cloning as a violation of biblical principles, specifically the command for men and women to multiply by consensual sexual union. Many see human cloning as unethical and even immoral since the technology is in its infancy and far from being perfected. These objectors argue that a large number of cloned animals have developed physical problems including severe arthritis, inexplicable obesity, and/or signs of excessively premature aging. It follows that to clone humans while the technology is still in its developmental stage would be unconscionable. Finally, some argue that in a very real sense the clone would part company with virtually all of humanity in that he or she would be a manufactured commodity, the product of a scientific procedure. Those critics argue that the clone would be condemned to lead his or her life as an echo or reflection of its donor parent.

Although fewer in number, most proponents of cloning are as passionate and varied in their support of the procedure as the majority is in its opposition. Civil libertarians claim that any ban on human cloning violates the constitutional right to bear children. They point out that the Constitution ensures the right to have children without specifying which procreative techniques must be used. Another common argument favoring human cloning revolves around the fact that the traditional family is rapidly changing. Supporters point to the increased use of day care centers for the children of single or working parents and the establishment of nuclear families by same-sex partners, either through adoption or artificial insemination, as illustrative of some of the new familial paradigms currently evolving. Proponents claim that cloning is simply a variation of these new sociological themes. And interestingly, there are some scientists who have even argued that cloning is a more efficient mode of human reproduction than is sexual reproduction.

There is one group, however, that opposes reproductive cloning while supporting cloning for medical purposes. These analysts argue that therapeutic cloning can offer many medical benefits. During the process of therapeutic cloning, the fetal clone would ultimately be aborted before moving beyond the blastocyst stage of embryonic growth. But prior to being aborted, the blastocyst would be used to harvest stem cells (undifferentiated cells which have not begun to specialize, that is, have not become muscle, liver, or other specific cells). It is believed that these cells, when introduced into the body of the donor parent, could possibly develop into healthy replacements for diseased or injured cells.

Throughout most of the twentieth century, popular depictions of cloning in general and human cloning in particular had been relegated to science fiction novels. From Aldous Huxley's *Brave New World* (1932), a disturbingly prophetic futuristic novel about state run "baby hatcheries," to Ira Levin's *The Boys from Brazil* (1976), a chilling depiction of multiple Adolf Hitler clones roaming the earth, cloning was limited to the fertile imagination of novelists. However as the twentieth century drew to a close and fiction became reality, the questioning and fear that frequently accompany many radical new technologies have become widespread. In *At Issue: Cloning* some of the more prominent arguments both for and against cloning are presented. To be sure, cloning is a form of reproduction that promises to generate controversy for much of the foreseeable future.

1

Human Cloning Is Dehumanizing

Leon R. Kass

Leon R. Kass is Addie Clark Harding Professor for the Committee on So-cial Thought at the University of Chicago.

Advocates of human cloning endorse the procedure for humanitarian reasons. However, most people are revolted at the prospect of human cloning since it violates many deeply held human values. There are also compelling rational arguments against human cloning: It constitutes unethical experimentation, it threatens identity and individuality, it turns procreation into manufacture, and it is a perversion of parenthood.

"To clone or not to clone a human being" is no longer a fanciful question. Success in cloning sheep, and also cows, mice, pigs, and goats, makes it perfectly clear that a fateful decision is now at hand: whether we should welcome or even tolerate the cloning of human beings. If recent newspaper reports are to be believed, reputable scientists and physicians have announced their intention to produce the first human clone. Their efforts may already be under way.

The gawking media

The media, gawking and titillating as is their wont, have been softening us up for this possibility by turning the bizarre into the familiar. In the four years since the birth of Dolly the cloned sheep, the tone of discussing the prospect of human cloning has gone from "Yuck" to "Oh?" to "Gee whiz" to "Why not?" The sentimentalizers, aided by leading bioethicists, have downplayed talk about eugenically cloning the beautiful and the brawny or the best and the brightest. They have taken instead to defending clonal reproduction for humanitarian or compassionate reasons: to treat infertility in people who are said to "have no other choice," to avoid the risk of severe genetic disease, to "replace" a child who has died. For the sake of these rare benefits, they would have us countenance the en-

Excerpted from "Preventing a Brave New World," by Leon R. Kass, *The New Republic*, May 21, 2001. Copyright © 2001 by *The New Republic*. Reprinted with permission.

tire practice of human cloning, the consequences be damned.

But we dare not be complacent about what is at issue, for the stakes are very high. Human cloning, though partly continuous with previous reproductive technologies, is also something radically new in itself and in its easily foreseeable consequences—especially when coupled with powers for genetic "enhancement" and germline genetic modification that may soon become available, owing to the recently completed Human Genome Project. I exaggerate somewhat, but in the direction of the truth: we are compelled to decide nothing less than whether human procreation is going to remain human, whether children are going to be made to order rather than begotten, and whether we wish to say yes in principle to the road that leads to the dehumanized hell of *Brave New World*. [Aldous Huxley's novel about a futuristic society in which babies are born in hatcheries.] . . .

How cloning works

What is cloning? Cloning, or asexual reproduction, is the production of individuals who are genetically identical to an already existing individual. The procedure's name is fancy—"somatic cell nuclear transfer"—but its concept is simple. Take a mature but unfertilized egg; remove or deactivate its nucleus; introduce a nucleus obtained from a specialized (somatic) cell of an adult organism. Once the egg begins to divide, transfer the little embryo to a woman's uterus to initiate a pregnancy. Since almost all the hereditary material of a cell is contained within its nucleus, the renucleated egg and the individual into which it develops are genetically identical to the organism that was the source of the transferred nucleus.

An unlimited number of genetically identical individuals—the group, as well as each of its members, is called "a clone"—could be produced by nuclear transfer. In principle, any person, male or female, newborn or adult, could be cloned, and in any quantity; and because stored cells can outlive their sources, one may even clone the dead. Since cloning requires no personal involvement on the part of the person whose genetic material is used, it could easily be used to reproduce living or deceased persons without their consent—a threat to reproductive freedom that has received relatively little attention.

> *We are compelled to decide . . . whether children are going to be made to order rather than begotten.*

Some possible misconceptions need to be avoided. Cloning is not Xeroxing: the clone of Bill Clinton, though his genetic double, would enter the world hairless, toothless, and peeing in his diapers, like any other human infant. But neither is cloning just like natural twinning: the cloned twin will be identical to an older, existing adult; and it will arise not by chance but by deliberate design; and its entire genetic makeup will be preselected by its parents and/or scientists. Moreover, the success rate of cloning, at least at first, will probably not be very high: [Dolly's creators] transferred two hundred seventy-seven adult nuclei into sheep eggs, implanted twenty-nine clonal embryos, and achieved the birth of only one live lamb clone.

For this reason, among others, it is unlikely that, at least for now, the practice would be very popular; and there is little immediate worry of mass-scale production of multicopies. Still, for the tens of thousands of people who sustain more than three hundred assisted-reproduction clinics in the United States and already avail themselves of in vitro fertilization and other techniques, cloning would be an option with virtually no added fuss. Panos Zavos, the Kentucky reproduction specialist who has announced his plans to clone a child, claims that he has already received thousands of e-mailed requests from people eager to clone, despite the known risks of failure and damaged offspring. Should commercial interests develop in "nucleus-banking," as they have in sperm-banking and egg-harvesting; should famous athletes or other celebrities decide to market their DNA the way they now market their autographs and nearly everything else; should techniques of embryo and germline genetic testing and manipulation arrive as anticipated, increasing the use of laboratory assistance in order to obtain "better" babies—should all this come to pass, cloning, if it is permitted, could become more than a marginal practice simply on the basis of free reproductive choice.

A revolting prospect

What are we to think about this prospect? Nothing good. Indeed, most people are repelled by nearly all aspects of human cloning: the possibility of mass production of human beings, with large clones of look-alikes, compromised in their individuality; the idea of father-son or mother-daughter "twins"; the bizarre prospect of a woman bearing and rearing a genetic copy of herself, her spouse, or even her deceased father or mother; the grotesqueness of conceiving a child as an exact "replacement" for another who has died; the utilitarian creation of embryonic duplicates of oneself, to be frozen away or created when needed to provide homologous tissues or organs for transplantation; the narcissism of those who would clone themselves, and the arrogance of others who think they know who deserves to be cloned; the Frankensteinian hubris to create a human life and increasingly to control its destiny; men playing at being God. Almost no one finds any of the suggested reasons for human cloning compelling, and almost everyone anticipates its possible misuses and abuses. And the popular belief that human cloning cannot be prevented makes the prospect all the more revolting.

Revulsion is not an argument; and some of yesterday's repugnances are today calmly accepted—not always for the better. In some crucial cases, however, repugnance is the emotional expression of deep wisdom, beyond reason's power completely to articulate it. Can anyone really give an argument fully adequate to the horror that is father-daughter incest (even with consent), or bestiality, or the mutilation of a corpse, or the eating of human flesh, or the rape or murder of another human being? Would anybody's failure to give full rational justification for his revulsion at those practices make that revulsion ethically suspect?

I suggest that our repugnance at human cloning belongs in this category. We are repelled by the prospect of cloning human beings not because of the strangeness or the novelty of the undertaking, but because we intuit and we feel, immediately and without argument, the violation of things that we rightfully hold dear. We sense that cloning represents a profound defilement of our given nature as procreative beings, and of the social relations built on this natural ground. We also sense that cloning is a radical form of child abuse. In this age in which everything is held to be permissible so long as it is freely done, and in which our bodies are regarded as mere instruments of our autonomous rational will, repugnance may be the only voice left that speaks up to defend the central core of our humanity. Shallow are the souls that have forgotten how to shudder.

Most people are repelled by nearly all aspects of human cloning.

Yet the repugnance need not stand naked before the bar of reason. The wisdom of our horror at human cloning can be at least partially articulated, even if this is finally one of those instances about which the heart has its reasons that reason cannot entirely know. I offer four objections to human cloning: that it constitutes unethical experimentation; that it threatens identity and individuality; that it turns procreation into manufacture (especially when understood as the harbinger of manipulations to come); and that it means despotism over children and perversion of parenthood. Please note: I speak only about so-called reproductive cloning, not about the creation of cloned embryos for research. The objections that may be raised against creating (or using) embryos for research are entirely independent of whether the research embryos are produced by cloning. What is radically distinct and radically new is reproductive cloning.

Any attempt to clone a human being would constitute an unethical experiment upon the resulting child-to-be. In all the animal experiments, fewer than two to three percent of all cloning attempts succeeded. Not only are there fetal deaths and stillborn infants, but many of the so-called "successes" are in fact failures. As has only recently become clear, there is a very high incidence of major disabilities and deformities in cloned animals that attain live birth. Cloned cows often have heart and lung problems; cloned mice later develop pathological obesity; other live-born cloned animals fail to reach normal developmental milestones.

Developmental defects

The problem, scientists suggest, may lie in the fact that an egg with a new somatic nucleus must re-program itself in a matter of minutes or hours (whereas the nucleus of an altered egg has been prepared over months and years). There is thus a greatly increased likelihood of error in translating the genetic instructions, leading to developmental defects some of which will show themselves only much later. (Note also that these induced abnormalities may also affect the stem cells that scientists hope to harvest from cloned embryos. Lousy embryos, lousy stem cells.) Nearly all scientists now agree that attempts to clone human beings carry massive risks of producing unhealthy, abnormal, and malformed children. What are we to do with them? Shall we just discard the ones that fall short of expectations? Considered opinion is today nearly unanimous, even among scientists: attempts at human cloning are irresponsible and unethical. We cannot ethically even get to know whether or not human cloning is feasible.

If it were successful, cloning would create serious issues of identity and individuality. The clone may experience concerns about his distinctive identity not only because he will be, in genotype and in appearance, identical to another human being, but because he may also be twin to the person who is his "father" or his "mother"—if one can still call them that. Unaccountably, people treat as innocent the homey case of intrafamilial cloning—the cloning of husband or wife (or single mother). They forget about the unique dangers of mixing the twin relation with the parent-child relation. (For this situation, the relation of contemporaneous twins is no precedent; yet even this less problematic situation teaches us how difficult it is to wrest independence from the being for whom one has the most powerful affinity.) Virtually no parent is going to be able to treat a clone of himself or herself as one treats a child generated by the lottery of sex. What will happen when the adolescent clone of Mommy becomes the spitting image of the woman with whom Daddy once fell in love? In case of divorce, will Mommy still love the clone of Daddy, even though she can no longer stand the sight of Daddy himself?

The popular belief that human cloning cannot be prevented makes the prospect all the more revolting.

Most people think about cloning from the point of view of adults choosing to clone. Almost nobody thinks about what it would be like to be the cloned child. Surely his or her new life would constantly be scrutinized in relation to that of the older version. Even in the absence of unusual parental expectations for the clone—say, to live the same life, only without its errors—the child is likely to be ever a curiosity, ever a potential source of déjà vu. Unlike "normal" identical twins, a cloned individual—copied from whomever—will be saddled with a genotype that has already lived. He will not be fully a surprise to the world: people are likely always to compare his doings in life with those of his alter ego, especially if he is a clone of someone gifted or famous. True, his nurture and his circumstance will be different; genotype is not exactly destiny. But one must also expect parental efforts to shape this new life after the original—or at least to view the child with the original version always firmly in mind. For why else did they clone from the star basketball player, the mathematician, or the beauty queen—or even dear old Dad—in the first place?

Genetic blueprint

Human cloning would also represent a giant step toward the transformation of begetting into making, of procreation into manufacture (literally, "handmade"), a process that has already begun with in vitro fertilization and genetic testing of embryos. With cloning, not only is the process in hand, but the total genetic blueprint of the cloned individual is selected and determined by the human artisans. To be sure, subsequent development is still according to natural processes; and the resulting children will be recognizably human. But we would be taking a major step into making man himself simply another one of the man-made things.

How does begetting differ from making? In natural procreation, human beings come together to give existence to another being that is formed exactly as we were, by what we are—living, hence perishable, hence aspiringly erotic, hence procreative human beings. But in clonal reproduction, and in the more advanced forms of manufacture to which it will lead, we give existence to a being not by what we are but by what we intend and design.

Let me be clear. The problem is not the mere intervention of technique, and the point is not that "nature knows best." The problem is that any child whose being, character, and capacities exist owing to human design does not stand on the same plane as its makers. As with any product of our making, no matter how excellent, the artificer stands above it, not as an equal but as a superior, transcending it by his will and creative prowess. In human cloning, scientists and prospective "parents" adopt a technocratic attitude toward human children: human children become their artifacts. Such an arrangement is profoundly dehumanizing, no matter how good the product.

Procreation dehumanized into manufacture is further degraded by commodification, a virtually inescapable result of allowing baby-making to proceed under the banner of commerce. Genetic and reproductive biotechnology companies are already growth industries, but they will soon go into commercial orbit now that the Human Genome Project has been completed. "Human eggs for sale" is already a big business, masquerading under the pretense of "donation." Newspaper advertisements on elite college campuses offer up to $50,000 for an egg "donor" tall enough to play women's basketball and with SAT scores high enough for admission to Stanford; and to nobody's surprise, at such prices there are many young coeds eager to help shoppers obtain the finest babies money can buy. (The egg and womb-renting entrepreneurs shamelessly proceed on the ancient, disgusting, misogynist premise that most women will give you access to their bodies, if the price is right.) Even before the capacity for human cloning is perfected, established companies will have invested in the harvesting of eggs from ovaries obtained at autopsy or through ovarian surgery, practiced embryonic genetic alteration, and initiated the stockpiling of prospective donor tissues. Through the rental of surrogate-womb services, and through the buying and selling of tissues and embryos priced according to the merit of the donor, the commodification of nascent human life will be unstoppable.

Confusing parent-child roles

Finally, the practice of human cloning by nuclear transfer—like other anticipated forms of genetically engineering the next generation—would enshrine and aggravate a profound misunderstanding of the meaning of having children and of the parent-child relationship. When a couple normally chooses to procreate, the partners are saying yes to the emergence of new life in its novelty—are saying yes not only to having a child, but also to having whatever child this child turns out to be. In accepting our finitude, in opening ourselves to our replacement, we tacitly confess the limits of our control.

Embracing the future by procreating means precisely that we are relinquishing our grip in the very activity of taking up our own share in what we hope will be the immortality of human life and the human species. This means that our children are not our children: they are not our property, they are not our possessions. Neither are they supposed to live our lives for us, or to live anyone's life but their own. Their genetic distinctiveness and independence are the natural foreshadowing of the deep truth that they have their own, never-before-enacted life to live. Though sprung from a past, they take an uncharted course into the future.

Cloning would create serious issues of identity and individuality.

Much mischief is already done by parents who try to live vicariously through their children. Children are sometimes compelled to fulfill the broken dreams of unhappy parents. But whereas most parents normally have hopes for their children, cloning parents will have expectations. In cloning, such overbearing parents will have taken at the start a decisive step that contradicts the entire meaning of the open and forward-looking nature of parent-child relations. The child is given a genotype that has already lived, with full expectation that this blueprint of a past life ought to be controlling the life that is to come. A wanted child now means a child who exists precisely to fulfill parental wants. Like all the more precise eugenic manipulations that will follow in its wake, cloning is thus inherently despotic, for it seeks to make one's children after one's own image (or an image of one's choosing) and their future according to one's will.

Is this hyperbolic? Consider concretely the new realities of responsibility and guilt in the households of the cloned. No longer only the sins of the parents, but also the genetic choices of the parents, will be visited on the children—and beyond the third and fourth generation; and everyone will know who is responsible. No parent will be able to blame nature or the lottery of sex for an unhappy adolescent's big nose, dull wit, musical ineptitude, nervous disposition, or anything else that he hates about himself. Fairly or not, children will hold their cloners responsible for everything, for nature as well as for nurture. And parents, especially the better ones, will be limitlessly liable to guilt. Only the truly despotic souls will sleep the sleep of the innocent.

The defenders of cloning are not wittingly friends of despotism. Quite the contrary. Deaf to most other considerations, they regard themselves mainly as friends of freedom: the freedom of individuals to reproduce, the freedom of scientists and inventors to discover and to devise and to foster "progress" in genetic knowledge and technique, the freedom of entrepreneurs to profit in the market. They want large-scale cloning only for animals, but they wish to preserve cloning as a human option for exercising our "right to reproduce"—our right to have children, and children with "desirable genes." As some point out, under our "right to reproduce" we already practice early forms of unnatural, artificial, and extra-marital reproduction, and we already practice early forms of eugenic choice. For that reason, they argue, cloning is no big deal.

We have here a perfect example of the logic of the slippery slope. The principle of reproductive freedom currently enunciated by the proponents of cloning logically embraces the ethical acceptability of sliding all the way down: to producing children wholly in the laboratory from sperm to term (should it become feasible), and to producing children whose entire genetic makeup will be the product of parental eugenic planning and choice. If reproductive freedom means the right to have a child of one's own choosing by whatever means, then reproductive freedom knows and accepts no limits.

Reproductive freedom

Proponents want us to believe that there are legitimate uses of cloning that can be distinguished from illegitimate but by their own principles no such limits can be found. (Nor could any such limits be enforced in practice: once cloning is permitted, no one ever need discover whom one is cloning and why.) Reproductive freedom, as they understand it, is governed solely by the subjective wishes of the parents-to-be. The sentimentally appealing case of the childless married couple is, on these grounds, indistinguishable from the case of an individual (married or not) who would like to clone someone famous or talented, living or dead. And the principle here endorsed justifies not only cloning but also all future artificial attempts to create (manufacture) "better" or "perfect" babies.

The "perfect baby," of course, is the project not of the infertility doctors, but of the eugenic scientists and their supporters, who, for the time being, are content to hide behind the skirts of the partisans of reproductive freedom and compassion for the infertile. For them, the paramount right is not the so-called right to reproduce, it is what the biologist Bentley Glass called, a quarter of a century ago, "the right of every child to be born with a sound physical and mental constitution, based on a sound genotype . . . the inalienable right to a sound heritage." But to secure this right, and to achieve the requisite quality control over new human life, human conception and gestation will need to be brought fully into the bright light of the laboratory, beneath which the child-to-be can be fertilized, nourished, pruned, weeded, watched, inspected, prodded, pinched, cajoled, injected, tested, rated, graded, approved, stamped, wrapped, sealed, and delivered. There is no other way to produce the perfect baby.

If you think that such scenarios require outside coercion or governmental tyranny, you are mistaken. Once it becomes possible, with the aid of human genomics, to produce or to select for what some regard as "better babies"—smarter, prettier, healthier, more athletic—parents will leap at the opportunity to "improve" their offspring. Indeed, not to do so will be socially regarded as a form of child neglect. Those who would ordinarily be opposed to such tinkering will be under enormous pressure to compete on behalf of their as yet unborn children—just as some now plan almost from their children's birth how to get them into Harvard.

Never mind that, lacking a standard of "good" or "better" no one can really know whether any such changes will truly be improvements.

Proponents of cloning urge us to forget about the science-fiction scenarios of laboratory manufacture or multiple-copy clones, and to focus only on the sympathetic cases of infertile couples exercising their reproductive rights. But why, if the single cases are so innocent, should multiplying their performance be so off-putting? (Similarly, why do others object to people's making money from that practice if the practice itself is perfectly acceptable?) The so-called science-fiction cases—say, *Brave New World*—make vivid the meaning of what looks to us, mistakenly, to be benign. They reveal that what looks like compassionate humanitarianism is, in the end, crushing dehumanization.

2

Human Cloning Is Unethical

Thomas A. Shannon

Thomas A. Shannon is professor of religion and social ethics at Worcester Polytechnic Institute, Worcester, Massachusetts.

Animals who were recently cloned have begun to manifest problems such as obesity and developmental delays. Although cloning has not been proven safe, cloning in general and the cloning of humans in particular continues to be advocated by many. There are several reasons for this including the fact that assisted reproduction has become a multi-billion-dollar-a-year industry. One issue, however, should remain paramount: Since cloning has not proven safe with animals, it would be unethical to clone humans.

The international team of Panayiotis Zavos, of the University of Kentucky, and Servino Antinori of Rome, Italy, and a group called the Raelians, who think humans were made by aliens using genetic technologies, have both announced that they are moving forward on the human cloning project. The Raelians will attempt to clone DNA from the deceased child of an American couple, and the international team has promised to clone a human in 2002.

For several years I have been predicting that the first place that human cloning would be done would be in an assisted reproduction clinic. The reasons are simple: such clinics are in the main unregulated—though four states prohibit human cloning; they have customers who are desperate to have a child with some genetic link to at least one partner; money does not seem to be an obstacle; and, when all other methods have failed, here is one last method to try.

I had assumed, however, that this would be done quietly and with a certain degree of discretion so as not to incite picketing at the clinic or professional disapproval. Little did I think that a major actor would be the Raelians (a group you can join if you send in a check for 3 percent of your post-tax income) and the international team. Nor did I foresee that the project would be announced with a great deal of fanfare. . . .

But this announcement has recently been complicated by reports from several scientists that cloned animals are beginning to manifest problems such as obesity, errors in the expression of the genes and developmental delay. The problems seem to be associated with the rapidity with which the clone is required to reprogram the genetic material, but the cause is not clear yet. What is clear is that there are problems and that some show up rather quickly, while others become apparent only later.

Although the technology of cloning has resulted in some clones, the argument that the technology works is facetious at best. Only a few clones have actually been produced, and a minimal number of these have been primates. Hundreds of embryos need to be produced to have a very few live births. Many clones do not survive or have to be euthanized because of various physical problems. Even after years of dedicated work and research, the Texas A&M facility has not succeeded in cloning Missy, a beloved dog whose owners generously funded the cloning project there. If this rush to application were done in any other area of medicine, I suspect the medical and scientific community, to say nothing of the federal government and consumer activist groups, would rise as one in protest at such improper scientific methods. Think of recent debates over drug trials. That such an unproved and unsafe method of assisted reproduction is being rushed to human use is simply wrong both scientifically and ethically.

Reasons why cloning is supported

There are, however, several interrelated reasons why this project seems to be going forward. First, in the U.S. autonomy has come to mean that I am entitled to do whatever I want. This is a variant of what Robert Bellah and his colleagues called "expressive individualism," the right to be who one wants to be and to seek those acts that both make me who I choose to be and that also express that self. This self stands apart from community and essentially knows no limits—except those imposed by one's imagination and credit line. This model of autonomy serves the cloning debate well by isolating any evaluation of desires and motives or of scientific efficacy from public debate.

Although the technology of cloning has resulted in some clones, the argument that the technology works is facetious at best.

Thus in the Raelian clinic, the DNA comes from a deceased child. How can others understand the parents' loss or their need or refuse them this last opportunity to see that particular configuration of DNA expressed? Others have expressed interest in cloning a parent or, a recurring theme, having a clone from which to harvest organs or perhaps bone marrow or stem cells. In this latter case it is important to note that two critical precedents have been set. In England, human cloning is permitted to obtain stem cells, with the proviso that the embryo will be terminated after two weeks. Additionally, in this country there have been two well-discussed cases of individuals using various assisted reproduction technologies to conceive children to use as bone marrow donors. Objections were rebuffed in the name of privacy and autonomy. The cloners will probably follow the same strategy.

Second, money counts. Assisted reproduction is a multi-billion-dollar-a-year industry. Funding is mainly private, though insurance will provide for some treatments. But in general, if one has the money up front, one can enter the clinic. Since the federal government does not at present subsidize cloning, monies will come from private individuals, private agencies or organizations like the Raelians. It would be better, I think, to have the federal government support research into cloning so that at least an institutional review board and/or some government agency would review it. Even modest oversight is better than none, especially with regard to safety issues.

The critical issue in the present cloning debate is the simple but fundamental issue of research ethics: the research has not been proven effective or safe on animal models.

Third, there are many infertile couples, as well as many gay and lesbian couples, who desire a child with a genetic link to one of the partners. For many of these people the current technologies have not worked. Or donor gametes are unacceptable because of the consequent genetic asymmetry between the partners. With cloning there is asymmetry, but it is from within the relation. If one is desperate for a child and all traditional attempts have failed, there is now one more option: cloning. With cloning, desperation joins up with the drive for progress, as well as for fame and fortune. And in a culture in which failure to use available technologies, no matter how risky, is equivalent to moral failure, eliminating this one last chance for a child with a genetic relation to one partner would be considered problematic, if not immoral.

Even though most people recognize that the clone is not the same person as the original, talk of replacement for a deceased child or a deceased parent or for one's self still continues. People talk of cloning as a form of secular immortality in that their DNA will march onward in a being at least genetically identical to them. One person reportedly said that he knew a clone of his mother would not be her, but he would like to give the clone a chance to experience all the things his mother was not able to experience because she grew up during the Depression. As if a fortune would be available to pursue such lifestyle options after paying for the cloning procedure! Such continuing misperceptions of what cloning will achieve reveal a profound ignorance of its outcome and perhaps of the process itself. How can informed consent be present here?

Why human cloning is unethical

Finally, one still hears the rhetoric of the clone as a source of spare parts or as a source of renewable parts like blood marrow. Notwithstanding the tragic circumstances that led at least two couples to avail themselves of assisted reproductive techniques to have a child precisely to use the child as a donor, such use reduces the child to a means and violates its dignity. Taking an organ from such a child would not only cause physical harm; it would also be a substantive violation of the child's integrity. Even if one is thinking of taking a kidney or part of the liver, or even bone marrow, the child is reduced to an object. Some have referred to this as neo-cannibalism, a label that, while perhaps a bit over the top, does make a point.

The critical issue in the present cloning debate is the simple but fundamental issue of research ethics: the research has not been proven effective or safe on animal models; therefore it is unethical to apply it to humans. It is not a violation of anyone's rights to insist, at the bare minimum, that the technique of cloning ought at least to be demonstrated as effective and safe before we rush into using it. However, in America we act first and think later—if at all. I think we have been and continue to be extremely lucky with the implementation of in vitro fertilization, which was also rushed to market without adequate animal trials. Maybe our luck will hold again, but shouldn't such decisions have a little more ethical mandate than just luck?

3

Cloning Is a Crime Against the Clone

George J. Annas

George J. Annas is Edward R. Utley Professor and Chair, Health Law Department, Boston University School of Public Health, and professor in the Boston University School of Medicine and School of Law.

Cloning represents a potential danger to the health of the clone. Moreover, the child-clone is condemned by its parent to be only an echo of the parent's life. In fact, cloning threatens to undermine those qualities which are unique to the individual, thereby debasing the clone's value and dignity as a human being. Ultimately, the clone can only view him- or herself as a manufactured product, not a person.

The chant is "cloning, cloning, cloning;" but the echo is "choice, choice, choice." From all the hoopla about human cloning as a human choice it would seem that cloning must be the most important scientific issue of our age. . . .

What is it that makes human cloning at once so appealing to a few and so repulsive to most? The answer, I think, can be found in Roman mythology: The cloning myth recalls Ovid's story of Echo and Narcissus.

The myth of Echo and Narcissus

Echo was a devastatingly beautiful woodland nymph who had one flaw, a fondness for chatter and an insistence on having the last word. One day Echo detained the goddess Juno with her conversation while Jove, who was cavorting with the nymphs, made his escape. When she discovered Echo's treachery, Juno cursed Echo, saying that she would henceforth only have the last word, but never the power to speak first. When Echo pursued Narcissus, a beautiful youth, she could not speak to him, but could only repeat his last words. He rejects her, and she pines away until her bones change to rock and nothing is left but her reply voice.

Narcissus, who was equally cruel to all, was ultimately cursed himself

22

and fell in love with his own reflection, which he admired greatly. Being unable to attain it, and being shunned by it, he was ultimately consumed by his passion for his reflection and pined away and died without obtaining his objective. In cloning terms, Narcissus can be seen as the clonee, and his reflection as his clone. Echo is the personification of the curse that the clonee passes to its clone: never to speak first, but always to repeat that which has gone before. The lesson from mythology is clear. Duplicating yourself is sterile, self-absorbed, and ultimately destructive. Moreover, creating a clone in your own image is to curse your child by condemning it to be only an echo.

The myth of Echo and Narcissus helps explain the almost universal horror at the prospect of human cloning that greeted the news in 1997 that embryologist Ian Wilmut had cloned a sheep, creating the genetic twin of an adult animal by reprogramming one of its somatic cells to act as the nucleus of an egg. He called the cloned lamb Dolly. This achievement was trumpeted as a scientific milestone. Debate about its implications for human cloning began immediately. Should this cloning technique be applied to humans? Who should decide and on what basis? Could human cloning be stopped? . . .

Creating a clone in your own image is to curse your child by condemning it to be only an echo.

We can learn a lot from the almost universal condemnation of human cloning and the international movement to ban it even if we never create a delayed genetic twin of an existing human. The most important things we can learn will likely be about life, not science, about values, not technique—things, like the prince's sheep, that are "invisible to the eye." The reason Ian Wilmut, and leaders around the world, called for a ban on applying cloning to humans is that the genetic replication of a human by cloning could radically alter the very definition of a human being by asexually replicating an existing or deceased human to produce the world's first human with a single genetic parent. The danger is that through human cloning we will lose something vital to our humanity, the uniqueness of every human. Cloning a human is also uniquely disturbing because it is the manufacture of a person made to order, it represents the potential loss of individuality and freedom, and it symbolizes science's unrestrained quest for mastery over nature for the sake of knowledge, power, and profits. Cloning can also be seen as undermining our very concepts of parenthood and parental responsibility, fertility and the status and value of children. . . .

The primary reason for banning human cloning was articulated by philosopher Hans Jonas in the early 1970s. He correctly noted that it does not matter that creating an exact duplicate of an existing person is physically and psychologically impossible. What matters is that a specific person is chosen to be cloned because of some characteristic or characteristics that person possesses (and, it is hoped, would be also possessed by the copy or clone). Jonas argued that cloning is a crime against the clone, the crime of depriving the clone of his or her "existential right to certain subjective terms of being"—most particularly, the "right to ignorance" of facts (about his original) that are likely to be "paralyzing for the spontaneity of becoming himself." This advance knowledge of what another has or has not accomplished with the clone's genome destroys the clone's "condition for authentic growth" in seeking to answer the fundamental question of all our beings, "Who am I?" Jonas continues:

> In brief [the clone] is antecedently robbed of the freedom which only under the protection of ignorance can thrive; and to rob a human-to-be of that freedom deliberately is an inexplicable crime that must not be committed even once. . . . The ethical command here entering the enlarged stage of our powers is: never to violate the right to that ignorance which is a condition of authentic action; or: to respect the right of each human life to find its own way and be a surprise to itself.

Jonas is correct. His argument applies only to a "delayed genetic twin" created from an existing human, not to genetic twins born at the same time. Even if one doesn't agree with Jonas, however, it is hypocritical to argue that a cloning technique that limits the liberty and choices of the resulting child can be justified on the basis that cloning expands the liberty and choices of would-be cloners. There is more at stake here than a hollow chant of choice.

For children, [cloning] is a form of child abuse, asexual child abuse.

To summarize, there are a series of reasons to ban human cloning. At the individual/family level there is the issue of human experimentation and the danger to the health of the clone. More important is the Echo-Narcissus syndrome: the parent who is so in love with him or herself that only a duplicate can fulfill his or her yearning for perfection (though this yearning can never be fulfilled and will only result in disappointment and death); and the child-clone who is cursed by its parent never to speak first, but only to be an echo of the parent's already-lived life. Cloning is simultaneously self-indulgent and self-destructive, and creates a child with a curse rather than a blessing. At the societal level cloning threatens to change the value of children by seeing them as products made to order, and all humans by undermining the uniqueness of every individual on which human dignity is based. Finally, at the species level, cloning changes the essence of human sexuality by abolishing the necessity of sexual reproduction, and with it our concepts of fertility and infertility.

French philosopher Michel Foucault writes that a passage from the great Argentine writer Jorge Luis Borges incited him to write an entire book exploring how science and society categorize or order things (*The Order of Things: An Archeology of the Human Sciences*). The passage quotes "a certain Chinese encyclopaedia" which divides animals into "(a) belonging to the Emperor, (b) embalmed, (c) tame, (d) sucking pigs, (e) sirens, (f) fabulous, (g) stray dogs, (h) included in the present classification, (i) frenzied, (j) innumerable, (k) drawn with a very fine camelhair brush, (l) et cetera, (m) having just broken the water pitcher, (n) that from a long way off look like flies." Borges did not add (but we can) "(o) cloned lambs," to his list. While each separate category is possible, Foucault (who writes that he could hardly stop laughing, albeit uneasily, at this ordering), observes that the "monstrous quality" in this categorization is the fact that "the common ground" on which a "meeting" of all of these animals would be possible "has itself been destroyed." We can thus never find a container to accommodate all of the entries. Put another way, "Absurdity destroys the *and* of the enumeration by making impossible the *in* where the things enumerated would be divided up."

Foucault was concerned with order (and disorder) and how society orders things to make meaning out of them. Foucault was not so much interested in proving the "truth" of life as he was in understanding why we think the way we do, and therefore what things seem normal or natural to us. The question of human cloning can usefully be examined from a categorical ordering perspective. More precisely, where does cloning "fit"? If we put cloning into the category of human reproduction, it will be in a list including such things as in vitro fertilization, embryo transfer, and artificial insemination, and we will judge it through the same lens that we have judged these other methods of "artificial reproduction." We could also put it in an ordered list of embryo manipulations, a list of scientific challenges, or a list of manufactured products. I think the list it fits into is a different list altogether. It is a list of types of asexual reproduction or replication. Other possibilities include a list of science fiction scenarios, a list of unnatural activities, and a list of crimes against humanity. The "list" into which we "fit" human cloning matters—and will likely determine how society both in the United States and the world deals with it.

An international ban

Cloning does not "fit into" the category of international crimes against humanity: (a) genocide, (b) murder, (c) torture, (d) slavery. Indeed, the international preoccupation with human cloning can be made to seem absurd in the company of these 20th-century horrors. Cloning would, however, fit well in a list of things that should never be done to children, including female genital mutilation, forced labor, unconsented-to reproduction, and sterilization. For children, it is a form of child abuse, asexual child abuse. An international ban on human cloning could be the first entry into a new category of international bioethics crimes: (a) human cloning. The clear implication would be that this category should grow and that effective transnational enforcement mechanisms should be created. On this view, which I think is the proper one, the remote prospect of human cloning provides the world community with a rare, perhaps unique, opportunity to agree that something that can be done scientifically to change the nature of humanity should not be done. This agreement could (and should) serve as a model for much wider international cooperation and regulation in the bioethics and genetics spheres generally.

4

The Judeo-Christian Argument Against Cloning

Stephen G. Post

At the time he wrote the following article, Stephen G. Post was associate professor of bioethics at the Center for Biomedical Ethics, Case Western Reserve University, Cleveland, Ohio.

There are numerous nonhypothetical criticisms which may be leveled at cloning. All of these, however, merely serve as a preamble to a single, overriding criticism: Cloning violates the structure of nature by encroaching upon God's domain. Procreation through the biblically sanctioned sexual union of man and woman is God's way, not cloning.

Some extremely hypothetical scenarios might be raised as if to justify human cloning. One might speculate, for example: If environmental toxins or pathogens should result in massive human infertility, human cloning might be imperative for species survival. But in fact recent claims about increasing male infertility worldwide have been found to be false. Some apologists for human cloning will insist on other strained "What if's." "What if" parents want to replace a dead child with an image of that child? "What if" we can enhance the human condition by cloning the "best" among us?

I shall offer seven unhypothetical criticisms of human cloning, but in no particular priority. The final criticism, however, is the chief one to which all else serves as preamble.

Although human cloning, if possible, is surely a novelty, it does not corner the market on newness. For millennia mothers and fathers have marveled at the newness of form in their newborns. I have watched newness unfold in our own two children, wonderful blends of the Amerasian variety. True, there probably is, as Freud argued, a certain narcissism in parental love, for we do see our own form partly reflected in the child, but, importantly, never entirely so. Sameness is dull, and as the French say, Vive la différence. It is possible that underlying the mystery of this newness of form is a creative wisdom that we humans will never quite equal.

This concern with the newness of each human form (identical twins are new genetic combinations as well) is not itself new. The scholar of constitutional law Laurence Tribe pointed out in 1978, for example, that human cloning could "alter the very meaning of humanity." Specifically, the cloned person would be "denied a sense of uniqueness." Let us remember that there is no strong analogy between human cloning and natural identical twinning, for in the latter case there is still the blessing of newness in the newborns, though they be two or more. While identical twins do occur naturally and are unique persons, this does not justify the temptation to impose external sameness more widely.

Surely no scientist would doubt that genetic diversity produced by procreation between a man and a woman will always be preferable to cloning.

Sidney Callahan, a thoughtful psychologist, argues that the random fusion of a couple's genetic heritage "gives enough distance to allow the child also to be seen as a separate other," and she adds that the egoistic intent to deny uniqueness is wrong because it is ultimately depriving. By having a different form from that of either parent, I am visually a separate creature, and this contributes to the moral purpose of not reducing me to a mere copy utterly controlled by the purposes of a mother or father.

Perhaps human clones will not look exactly alike anyway, given the complex factors influencing genetic imprinting, as well as environmental factors affecting gene expression. But they will look more or less the same, rather than more or less different.

Surely no scientist would doubt that genetic diversity produced by procreation between a man and a woman will always be preferable to cloning, because procreation reduces the possibility for species annihilation through particular diseases or pathogens. Even in the absence of such pathogens, cloning means the loss of what geneticists describe as the additional hybrid vigor of new genetic combination.

Making males reproductively obsolete

Cloning requires human eggs, nuclei and uteri, all of which can be supplied by women. This makes males reproductively obsolete. This does not quite measure up to Shulamith Firestone's notion that women will only be able to free themselves from patriarchy through the eventual development of the artificial womb, but of course, with no men available, patriarchy ends—period.

Cloning, in the words of Richard McCormick, S.J., [Society of Jesus i.e. Jesuit priest] "would involve removing insemination and fertilization from the marriage relationship, and it would also remove one of the partners from the entire process." Well, removal of social fatherhood is already a fait accompli in a culture of illegitimacy chic, and one to which some fertility clinics already marvelously contribute through artificial insemination by donor for single women. Removing male impregnators from the procreative dyad would simply drive the nail into the coffin of fatherhood, unless one thinks that biological and social fatherhood are utterly disconnected. Social fatherhood would still be possible in a world of clones, but this will lack the feature of participation in a continued biological lineage that seems to strengthen social fatherhood in general.

Under my thumb: cookie cutters and power

It is impossible to separate human cloning from concerns about power. There is the power of one generation over the external form of another, imposing the vicissitudes of one generation's fleeting image of the good upon the nature and destiny of the next. One need only peruse the innumerable texts on eugenics written by American geneticists in the 1920's to understand the arrogance of such visions.

One generation always influences the next in various ways, of course. But when one generation can, by the power of genetics, in the words of C.S. Lewis, "make its descendants what it pleases, all men who live after it are the patients of that power." What might our medicalized culture's images of human perfection become? In Lewis' words again, "For the power of Man to make himself what he pleases means, as we have seen, the power of some men to make other men what they please."

A certain amount of negative eugenics by prenatal testing and selective abortion is already established in American obstetrics. Cloning extends this power from the negative to the positive, and it is therefore even more foreboding.

This concern with overcontrol and overpower may be overstated because the relationship between genotype and realized social role remains highly obscure. Social role seems to be arrived at as much through luck and perseverance as anything else, although some innate capacities exist as genetically informed baselines.

Born to be harvested

One hears regularly that human clones would make good organ donors. But we ought not to presume that anyone wishes to give away body parts. The assumption that the clone would choose to give body parts is completely unfounded. Forcing such a harvest would reduce the clone to a mere object for the use of others. A human person is an individual substance of a rational nature not to be treated as object, even if for one's own narcissistic gratification, let alone to procure organs. I have never been convinced that there are any ethical duties to donate organs.

The problem of mishaps

Dolly the celebrated ewe represents one success out of 277 embryos, nine of which were implanted. Only Dolly survived. While I do not wish to address here the issue of the moral status of the entity within the womb, suffice it to note that in this country there are many who would consider proposed research to clone humans as far too risky with regard to induced genetic defects. Embryo research in general is a matter of serious moral debate in the United States, and cloning will simply bring this to a head.

As one recent British expert on fertility studies writes, "Many of the animal clones that have been produced show serious developmental abnormalities, and, apart from ethical considerations, doctors would not run the medico-legal risks involved."

Sources of the self

Presumably no one needs to be reminded that the self is formed by experience, environment and nurture. From a moral perspective, images of human goodness are largely virtue-based and therefore characterological. Aristotle and Thomas Aquinas believed that a good life is one in which, at one's last breath, one has a sense of integrity and meaning. Classically the shaping of human fulfillment has generally been a matter of negotiating with frailty and suffering through perseverance in order to build character. It is not the earthen vessels, but the treasure within them that counts. A self is not so much a genotype as a life journey. Martin Luther King Jr. was getting at this when he said that the content of character is more important than the color of skin.

"Many of the animal clones that have been produced show serious developmental abnormalities."

The very idea of cloning tends to focus images of the good self on the physiological substrate, not on the journey of life and our responses to it, some of them compensations to purported "imperfections" in the vessel. The idea of the designer baby will emerge, as though external form is as important as the inner self.

Respect for nature and nature's God

In the words of Jewish bioethicist Fred Rosner, cloning goes so far in violating the structure of nature that it can be considered as "encroaching on the Creator's domain." Is the union of sex, marriage, love and procreation something to dismiss lightly?

Marriage is the union of female and male that alone allows for procreation in which children can benefit developmentally from both a mother and father. In the Gospel of Mark, Jesus draws on ancient Jewish teachings when he asserts, "Therefore what God has joined together, let no man separate." Regardless of the degree of extendedness in any family, there remains the core nucleus: wife, husband and children. Yet the nucleus can be split by various cultural forces (e.g., infidelity as interesting, illegitimacy as chic), poverty, patriarchal violence and now cloning.

A cursory study of the Hebrew Bible shows the exuberant and immensely powerful statements of Genesis 1, in which a purposeful, ordering God pronounces that all stages of creation are "good." The text proclaims, "So God created humankind in his image, in the image of God he created them, male and female he created them" (Gen. 1: 27). This God commands the couple, each equally in God's likeness, to "be fruitful and multiply." The divine prototype was thus established at the very outset of the Hebrew Bible: "Therefore a man leaves his father and his mother and clings to his wife, and they become one flesh" (Gen. 2: 24).

The dominant theme of Genesis 1 is creative intention. God creates, and what is created procreates, thereby ensuring the continued presence of God's creation. The creation of man and woman is good in part because it will endure. Catholic natural law ethicists and Protestant proponents of "orders of creation" alike find divine will and principle in the passages of Genesis 1.

Christians simply cannot and must not underestimate the threat of human cloning to unravel what is both naturally and eternally good.

A major study on the family by the Christian ethicist Max Stackhouse suggests that just as the pre-Socratic philosophers discovered still valid truths about geometry, so the biblical authors of Chapters One and Two of Genesis "saw something of the basic design, purpose, and context of life that transcends every sociohistorical epoch." Specifically, this design includes "fidelity in communion" between male and female oriented toward "generativity" and an enduring family the precise social details of which are worked out in the context of political economies.

Christianity appropriated the Hebrew Bible and had its origin in a Jew from Nazareth and his Jewish followers. The basic contours of Christian thought on marriage and family therefore owe a great deal to Judaism. These Hebraic roots that shape the words of Jesus stand within Malachi's prophetic tradition of emphasis on inviolable monogamy. In Mk. 10: 2–12 we read:

> The Pharisees approached and asked, "Is it lawful for a husband to divorce his wife?" They were testing him. He said to them in reply, "What did Moses command you?" They replied, "Moses permitted him to write a bill of divorce and dismiss her." But Jesus told them, "Because of the hardness of your hearts he wrote you this commandment. But from the beginning of creation, God made them male and female. For this reason a man shall leave his father and mother (and be joined to his wife), and the two shall become one flesh. So they are no longer two but one flesh. Therefore what God has joined together, no human being must separate." In the house the disciples again questioned him about this. He said to them, "Whoever divorces his wife and marries another commits adultery against her; and if she divorces her husband and marries another, she commits adultery."

Here Jesus quotes Gen. 1: 27 ("God made them male and female") and Gen. 2: 24 ("the two shall become one flesh").

Christians side with the deep wisdom of the teachings of Jesus, manifest in a thoughtful respect for the laws of nature that reflect the word of God. Christians simply cannot and must not underestimate the threat of human cloning to unravel what is both naturally and eternally good.

5

Arguments Favoring Human Cloning Are Wrong

Lane P. Lester and James C. Hefley

Lane P. Lester has taught at the University of Tennessee at Chattanooga, at Purdue University where he earned a Ph.D. in genetics in 1971, and at Liberty University. He is a professor of biology at Emmanuel College in Franklin Springs, Georgia. James C. Hefley is adjunct professor at Hannibal-LaGrange College in Hannibal, Missouri. An author of over seventy books, he holds a Ph.D. in mass communications from the University of Tennessee.

Human cloning is a serious and frightening prospect for the future and therefore should be avoided. Despite this, advocates have proffered numerous arguments in support of human cloning since the procedure first surfaced. The arguments include: Cloning perpetuates genius, it can provide specialized classes of people, it can improve human genetics, it can prevent genetic disease, it can provide body parts, and it is a door to immortality for donors. However, all of the major arguments favoring cloning can be readily refuted.

S cientific meetings aren't always the stuffy sessions they're made out to be. At a March 1977 forum of the National Academy of Sciences in Washington, D.C., the subject was cloning. A learned researcher was lecturing when a band of objectors suddenly began chanting, "We shall not be cloned!" Swarming onto the stage, they unfurled a banner proclaiming: "We will create the perfect race—Adolf Hitler." And that was more than twenty years ago.

Scientific debate about cloning is usually a little more orderly but still spirited. Rarely will you find anyone neutral about whether human beings should be cloned, especially with the recent advances in that direction. Molecular biologist Leon Kass once served as executive secretary of the Committee on Life Sciences and Social Policy for the National Academy of Sciences. He told an annual meeting of the Association of American Law Schools in Chicago that a human being should not be cloned

31

even once. The ability to do so, he said, is not a justifiable reason. Princeton's Dr. Paul Ramsey, the theologian most often quoted by those against cloning, said prospective mishaps in cloning experiments that would inevitably result in the formation and destruction of malformed embryos call for a moral prohibition.

Stanford's Dr. Joshua Lederberg and Joseph Fletcher, of "situation ethics" fame, have been two of the main cheerleaders for human cloning. Lederberg has never advocated doing away with the old-fashioned way of having babies, but he does think that clonal reproduction should have equal opportunity. Fletcher's dictum is that humanity itself must be in control of human evolution. This is typical of the way evolutionary humanists think. Humanity, they believe, is not here by design and special creation but only by evolutionary processes. Since there is no creator, sustainer, and controller of the universe, we must look out for ourselves and work out our own destiny. . . .

Cloning is a serious, even frightening prospect for the future. I'm going to try to refute the stated advantages of human cloning cited by those who think it would be a good and daring thing to do.

Cloning is a great way to perpetuate genius

How about a hundred Einsteins, two dozen Picassos, ten or twelve Mozarts, a dozen Shakespeares, and a lifetime supply of Carusos? The fact is that we cannot clone people who are long dead and buried. Even if we exhumed their bodies and searched for live cells, there would be none to find. The way we bury people, the cells of the deceased expire pretty fast.

Actually, the promoters of cloning advocate selecting a few of the "greatest" men and women now living for cloning. But who would select the candidates? If the cloning were to be done by a government or university team of biologists, a committee would probably be named. What criteria would they use? Would Christian faith be a plus or minus? Right now, evolutionary humanists are pretty much in control of our higher educational system, the textbook publishing houses, and the government bureaucracies that fund most of the scientific research. I doubt if they'd like a dozen more Billy Grahams or Jerry Falwells.

Prospective mishaps in cloning experiments that would inevitably result in the formation and destruction of malformed embryos call for a moral prohibition.

Even if an exact chip off the brilliant block of Albert Einstein could be cloned, there is no guarantee that his "twin" would be as smart as the original. Scientists continue to debate the relative powers of nature and nurture in shaping a life. Is heredity or environment more important? Natural intelligence or the motivation to learn? We all know gifted people who choose to dissipate their endowments through laziness, worthless hobbies, drug use, or some other desecration of talent. Furthermore, the clonal "son" or "daughter" of a genius would live in another era. The time and setting in which we live affect the way we respond to challenges. Also, numerous studies have shown that talent and accomplishments tend to run in families. Children of doctors are more likely to become physicians, for example. Children born and nurtured by parents who value learning are more apt to graduate from college. There are exceptions, of course, but in general this is the way it is. Some studies have shown that the home has more influence on a child's development than today's public school.

The idea of cloning genius is not heaven-sent. It comes from another source.

Unless adopted, clonal children would not have normal family lives. How would they fare in peer relationships? The "parents" of clones might decide to keep their little group of identicals together. How would it be for three or four identicals to grow up in the same household? Suppose clonal children knew they were the offspring of geniuses. How would they be affected by the social pressure to measure up? Any youth counselor can tell you about the agony some kids endure in trying to meet parental expectations.

There's a related issue to the cloning of genius that I must mention. This is the possibility of a megalomaniac having himself cloned. Or a deranged scientist deciding to clone his beloved despot. If you want a graphic picture of the horrors this might bring about, read Ira Levin's novel *The Boys from Brazil*. The book opens with former Nazi officials being given orders to commit a bizarre series of murders of sixty-five-year-old adoptive fathers. As the plot unfolds, Nazi hunter Yakov Liebermann follows the trail to Frieda Maloney, a former concentration camp guard, who was hired by an organization to get a job with an adoption agency so she could look at their files. Following instructions, she selected applications of would-be adoptive parents in which the husband was born between 1908 and 1912 and the wife between 1931 and 1935. Each husband had to have a civil service job, and both parents had to be white Christians with a Nordic racial background. At regular intervals, the organization gave her babies to place with these families. She thought they were the illegitimate children of German girls and South American boys and innocently went along with the scheme. Actually, they were the progeny of Hitler, cloned from cells taken from his body in 1943 and preserved for future cloning by the evil Nazi physician, Dr. Josef Mengele. The babies—ninety-four little Hitlers—were conceived in Dr. Mengele's lab and carried to term by Brazilian Indian tribeswomen.

Dr. Mengele planned for them to have parents similar to the Fuehrer's. Hitler's father was a civil servant, a customs officer. He was fifty-two when Adolf was born; his wife, twenty-nine. The father died at sixty-five when Adolf was almost fourteen. In the book, the adoptive fathers were killed systematically about the time of their sixty-fifth birthdays, when their adopted sons were almost fourteen. In a chilling scene near the end of the novel, Mengele meets one of the boys. "You were born from a cell of the greatest man who ever lived!" he shouts. "*Reborn!* . . . You're the living duplicate of the greatest man in all history!" I don't want to give the rest of the story away. Read the book, and you'll find the boy's response intriguing.

The idea of cloning genius is not heaven-sent. It comes from another source.

Cloning can provide soldier and servant classes of people

Joseph Fletcher once suggested that top soldiers might be cloned to fight soldiers of a tyrannical power. As far out as this sounds, I find it interesting that he admits that despots will use cloning. This isn't science fiction. If one person can be cloned, an army can be so produced. Presumably, the "parents" would all be fine physical specimens with keen minds and quick reflexes to pass on to their clones.

The raw material could be warehoused in special clone banks. Donor inseminators are already using sperm banks. Remember Robert Graham, who died about the time Dolly the sheep was in the news? Several years ago, he set up a special bank in California to house the sperm of Nobel prize winners. Columnist Ellen Goodman says as many as 218 children have already been born "with sperm from those little narcissus bulbs."

Soldiers are not the only special group clonal crusaders have in mind. Some universities are so hard up for football talent that they might even guarantee alumni that funding for cloning projects would result in winning teams. Also, special clones could be produced for other jobs that ordinary humans find distasteful or dangerous. Scientists would be cloning people to be used as slaves and work animals. They would look like ordinary human beings, yet they would be treated as subhuman. They would have no more rights than animals. I can't imagine any humane person backing such a program.

Cloning can improve the genetics of the human race

Selective breeding of subjects has been practiced by slave holders from Roman times to the pre–Civil War American South. They simply ordered strong, intelligent men and women to sleep together, even if they were betrothed or married to other people. Hitler's scientists probably never considered human cloning possible when they set out to purify the "Aryan race." They did it the way previous tyrants had. If the Nazis had known how to clone, they certainly wouldn't have gone to the trouble of bringing in young Aryan men and women for mating.

Cloning will likely bring about a genetic disadvantage for race improvement, depending on how much the procedure is used. The cloning of millions of people will diminish the variability resulting from the heterosexual mixing of genes. Generally, the combining of two different heredities will produce a stronger progeny. For this reason a farmer buys hybrid seeds instead of using his own from a single stock. Another problem will become clearer as I move forward. Everyone possesses harmful genes that result from mutation. Cloning will keep these genes in circulation. Couldn't persons with problem genes be identified and classified "4-F," like draft rejects were in World War II? Probably not, unless some physical evidence of genetic disease is present. That type of person wouldn't be considered by doctors in a despotic nation.

Dr. Lederberg, at Stanford University, conceded that wholesale clonal reproduction could lead into an "evolutionary cul-de-sac" with no chance of genetic improvement. A quarter century ago he proposed "tempered clonality," which would allow for both cloning and heterosexual reproduction. He thought then that selected cloning could improve a race by adding "better" people. This would require a government regulatory agency with two major responsibilities: (1) to select the candidates for cloning, and (2) to keep the clonal people from mating with other clonal people or the choice offspring of heterosexual mating. Allowing clonal people to mate would destroy any racial "benefits" to be gained by the selective use of cloning.

With human nature as it is, I don't see the latter as possible. A clonal person would have the same urges as we all do, and he or she would find a partner. The "crime" would be found out when the child was born. Would the violators be punished for breaking the law of the clones? Would the innocent child be killed?

Cloning can prevent genetic disease in a selected posterity

This argument also sounds good on the surface. The genetic engineers would simply pick out the best "stock" for cloning. Genetic disease caused by the mixing of certain heredities would be avoided. However, this is not as fail-safe as it might seem. Clonal people would still be susceptible to mutations or mistakes in the replication of cells. They would also be affected by environmental influences that may bring out previously unknown genetic disease. One of the many genetic diseases that can remain undetected until activated by environment and lifestyle is Herniske-Korsakoff syndrome. An enzyme called transketolase, which regulates or filters vitamin B_1 to the brain, is missing from the cells. People with the defect don't get enough B_1 to prevent the disorder from spreading. Without B_1 supplements, victims go hopelessly insane.

Cloning will merely perpetuate such genetic defects. It offers no panacea for the elimination of genetic disease.

Clones can exchange body parts and experience enhanced social communion

This is one of Dr. Lederberg's key planks in his platform for cloning. Since all clonal persons are identical twins, a number of donors could be available for organ transplants. As identical twins, they would share a closeness and understanding that would facilitate harmony and peace, enabling them to work together cohesively. This assumes that the cloned individuals would be willing to make the sacrifices required in donating organs. It assumes they would be free from self-centeredness, jealousy, greed, and other failings of ordinary men and women. Utopian experiments have always failed to create perfection among ordinary people. I cannot believe that members of a clone would live together in sweet communion. Evolutionary humanists ignore the sin factor that inevitably spoils man-made Edens. "The crude evidence in human experience," said Dr. Paul Ramsey, "does not lend unequivocal support to the expectation that 'intimate communication' would be increased." To the contrary, Ramsey suggested that "animosity in personal relations might be heightened."

Ramsey further indicated that the struggle for selfhood and identity in a clone could be intense. "Growing up as a twin is difficult enough. . . . Who then would want to be the son or daughter of his twin? To mix the parental and the twin relation might well be psychologically disastrous for the young." Personal and psychological independence, Ramsey projected, might be impossible to achieve for children who are the exact copy of their one "parent."

Cloning can provide a genotype of a family member

Advocates of cloning suggest that couples unable to have children together might prefer a cloned child to one by artificial insemination, since a third person would not be involved. Here, too, there could be an identity problem, unless the child was never told of his or her true parentage. Even so, the amazing likeness between the child and one of the parents would be obvious when the child looked in the mirror. Cloning to preserve the genotype of a departed loved one will require that the necessary cells be removed before death. Biologists can already keep cells alive in a laboratory culture for an indefinite time. If and when human cloning is accomplished, such "restoration" of the dead will be possible. Dead men can even now sire children through artificial insemination, using sperm donated and frozen while they were alive.

Such a possibility raises a hard question. Whose child will the offspring be? The scientist who does the cloning, the relative who pays for the act, or the deceased donor?

If so, it will be only for those who can afford to pay for the cloning. But let's suppose cloning for this purpose is made available to whoever desires it. We've all known parents who seek to relive their youth through a son or daughter. This can create serious psychological problems in the offspring. No youth should be burdened to live the life of a selfish parent. Furthermore, there is absolutely no evidence that human consciousness can be transferred to a clonal descendant. The genes will be substantially the same, but the memory and thought patterns of the parent will not be reimplanted. . . .

Cloning can increase scientific knowledge about human reproduction

Hitler's scientists increased their knowledge by studying human brains taken from the skulls of undesirables killed in pruning people from the Aryan race. This, of course, did not justify the murder of these innocent people. Unlawful and inhumane experiments on other human beings have occurred, even in the United States. I don't doubt that some American scientists have worked with aborted, live human fetuses. Their goal may be to learn more about genetic disease, but the work is still wrong—shockingly, appallingly wrong—and a gross violation of the rights of the unborn. I have already said that a cloned offspring, prenatal or postnatal, will be a person. He or she should not be treated like a laboratory animal.

6

Human Cloning Will Distort Parenthood

Sondra Wheeler

Sondra Wheeler is the Martha Ashby Carr Professor of Christian Ethics at Wesley Theological Seminary in Washington, D.C. She is the author of Stewards of Life: Bioethics and Pastoral Care, *as well as numerous articles concerning the intersection of bioethics and Christian theology.*

The parent-child relationship is the most fundamental of all human relationships. Cloning threatens the very fabric of that relationship by creating an offspring who is basically an engineered product. In essence, the child becomes a commodity and the parent a consumer. By fundamentally altering the relationship between parent and child, cloning can lead to a basic distortion of parenting.

The immediate furor sparked by the birth of Dolly the cloned sheep has now died down. We have turned our attention to other things, perhaps revealing that as a nation we have the cultural equal of attention deficit disorder. More deeply, I suspect, we have run out of things to say about human cloning, and this is the reflection of our lack of a shared and generally available language in which to talk about our hopes, fears, and intuitions concerning the control of human genetic inheritance.

Discussion continues, mostly in specialized settings, academic and professional contexts, or scientific and philosophical journals. There, experts debate the possible benefits and foreseeable risks of cloning applications that would result in the birth of a child who was the deliberate genetic copy of some existing template, whether of one of the rearing parents or of some other person. These discussions are important. It is quite reasonable to look to scientists and ethicists to help us understand the technical possibilities, and to frame the questions that the fast-maturing discipline of bioethics teaches us to ask about their moral acceptability. But such debates among specialists are not sufficient.

All proposed forays into human genetic engineering are significant because they have the capacity, by changing what we *do*, to change what we *mean* by terms as basic as mother and father. Accepting such new practices requires us to make a subtle shift in what we understand and intend in entering into the most fundamental of all human relationships, that between parent and child. There is no academic specialty in what it means to be the fruit of the previous generation or the progenitors of the next. No degrees are available that confer the wisdom necessary to judge the terms on which, or the ends *for* which, we ought to undertake to determine the genetic complement of those other human beings whom we will call our children. Moreover, whether they realize it or not, there are no human beings on the planet to whom the moral character of these basic social ties is irrelevant. Therefore it is important to continue the discussion in the broadest possible terms and among the widest possible segment of the society that stands to be affected by these developments. . . .

Revisiting the arguments for cloning

Positive arguments for human reproductive cloning are actually hard to come by. Those who support the pursuit of that goal generally do so for what might be called negative reasons (that is, they find no convincing reasons to ban the practice) rather than for the sake of some particular good cloning is expected to bring about. There are, in fact, a number of rationales for supporting cloning of preimplantation embryos as a tool in basic and clinical research, and a wide range of possible therapeutic benefits projected to come from such research. But these do not depend upon implanting cloned embryos or the result of nuclear transfers and bringing them to term, and thus do not fall into the category of reproductive cloning. Just to be clear, there are also serious arguments against these research protocols, rooted in respect for the embryo as a form of nascent human life that should not be manipulated and discarded. These objections, however, are not particular to procedures that involve cloning, applying as well to any creation of human embryos not destined for implantation.

Positive arguments for human reproductive cloning are actually hard to come by.

Some of the arguments that have been made in favor of reproductive cloning proceed on libertarian grounds, that only direct and demonstrated harm to a recognized other should limit individual autonomy. These depend on the supposition that the procedure can be made safe for the cloned child-to-be and for the gestating mother, and on the prior supposition that failures on the way to such a technical development do not harm any being who is morally eligible for protection. On these premises, libertarians argue that no one has the right to limit what researchers or prospective cloners wish to do. Cloning is to be supported because it might provide a way for prospective parents to obtain the offspring they want, whether that means overcoming disease or just exercising "quality control." The substantive good in view in this position is thus individual liberty.

Most people do not find such arguments for unconstrained cloning convincing on the face of it, for the same reason that they do not find libertarian arguments in favor of ending tax support for public education convincing. It is entirely too evident how much common stake we all have in the bearing and upbringing of children, who are after all destined to be our neighbors and inheritors, to suppose that such practices should be matters of purely private judgment. Even those who have supported some uses of human cloning have generally recognized that proposals must pass greater public scrutiny than this.

More appealing to some have been arguments based on benefits that might be obtained using this technique for individuals in particular circumstances. Rabbi Moshe Tendler, for example, envisions a case in which someone, all of whose relatives were killed in the Holocaust, is unable to produce gametes, but has a great stake in continuing his or her family line. The use of nuclear transfer cloning technology might allow this person to have posterity by first producing a genetic twin. Ronald Cole-Turner asks whether a couple who loses a late-term pregnancy at a point when they can no longer conceive might be justified in cloning the dead fetus to obtain a child who was genetically related to both of them. A number of commentators have proposed that cloning might enable couples who carry certain serious genetic defects to be certain of not passing these to their offspring. And a few have noted that cloning could allow lesbian couples to have children genetically related to them and to no one else, extending the contemporary notion of a right to procreate to those now excluded by biology. These are not, of course, routine circumstances, and such unusual scenarios raise the question of whether "hard cases" make better ethics than they do law. But the exploration of quandaries can help to clarify what is at the heart of our intuitions and our considered judgments and help us articulate what might be at stake in our decisions. . . .

Arguments against cloning

Arguments against the moral permissibility of cloning can also be divided into types. The first and simplest type argues on grounds of scientific safety and reliability that such experimental procedures are too risky to apply to human beings. Those who would make this the grounds for an ongoing or permanent ban contend that any research that would reduce the uncertainty is morally prohibited because it would involve helpless and unconsenting subjects in high-risk, non-therapeutic research. They deny that animal studies can ever give us sufficient confidence to justify proceeding to human trials.

Many have objected to cloning because they see a threat to human dignity and individuality in a technique that creates a genetic replica of an existing genotype. Popular commentators have raised questions about the personal identity, value, and social status to be accorded a clone. While others counter that cloning poses no greater threat to genetic uniqueness than natural twinning, opponents point to a distinction between what one accepts as a random event and what one sets out to do. They also point out that it makes a difference if one of the twins is a deliberately chosen template, already fully developed, who may function socially as the "parent" of the other.

Related but distinct are the concerns of those who worry about com-

promising genetic diversity in favor of the replication of a few highly val-
ued genotypes. Along with the biological risks if it were to be done on a
large scale, cloning raises philosophical questions about human nature
and the value of human differences. Further along this same trajectory of
concern for human freedom and dignity, some have speculated about the
uses of cloning to create whole categories of people specially adapted for
some social purpose, ranging from soldiers to worker drones to sources of
"replacement parts" for their cloners. Some have proposed these possibilities with full seriousness as moral barriers to the application of this technique to human beings. Whatever the criteria or motives for selection,
the replication of a desirable genotype has seemed to many to be a fatal
step toward treating infants as commodities.

Changing the focus

Common to all these objections is the fear of making a human being a
merely instrumental good, a being created at someone else's direction
and to his or her specifications to fulfill a human purpose outside the
child's own flourishing. This is seen as a basic violation of the duty of respect for persons, which forbids treating them solely as means to other
ends, rather than as ends in themselves. This concern is evident even
among those thinkers, both religious and secular, who do not find the
asexual character of replication and the lack of genetic uniqueness compelling arguments against cloning. Ted Peters, for example, untroubled by
these issues, nevertheless worries that "reproduction will come to look
more and more like production . . . with quality control and babies will
come to look more and more like products." Karen Lebacqz, in considering sympathetically whether cloning might serve social justice by extending the putative right to a genetically related child to disadvantaged
groups, asks a more basic question: "Is there something fundamentally
flawed with the notion that children must be genetically ours? Is the very
language of 'rights' out of place when it comes to procreation and families?" She concludes: "Our individualistic, 'rights'-based assumptions
about families and procreation need to be challenged, and fundamentally
new understandings of family need to be developed."

*Popular commentators have raised questions about
the personal identity, value, and social status to be
accorded a clone.*

Although there are aspects of both Peters's and Lebacqz's analyses
with which I would take issue, they share a central insight that seems to
me exactly right: it is the moral character of human relationships within
the family, rather than simply the mechanics of embryo generation or the
raw biochemistry of genetic identity, that is the heart of the matter. Even
the most sensitive analysis of the dignity of procreation as a natural
process, or the respect to be accorded the human embryo as an individual entity, will leave something crucial out of the picture, namely, the social practice of parenting as a central human activity. This returns me to

the matters with which I began, with the implications of reproductive cloning for how we think about family life, and how we understand and protect the bearing and rearing of children as a moral practice.

Welcoming the stranger: contingency, uncertainty, and the virtues of parenting

In trying to think morally about a possibility for which there is no precedent, it sometimes helps to think carefully about the familiar pattern it proposes to replace. This can be surprisingly difficult to do, for the same familiarity that makes us comfortable also makes us blind to important features of our ordinary experience. This makes it necessary to say some very obvious things about the experience of becoming a parent.

Ian Wilmut, Dolly's scientific progenitor, speaks of people having children in what he calls "the ordinary, fun way." The truth is, it is fun; not just the lovemaking, but pregnancy itself. Despite its many discomforts, pregnancy is a perennial wonder, as the child within makes its presence more and more known and felt, as the curiosity and anticipation grow, and parents ponder a thousand variations on the question, "I wonder who it will be?" For the fact is, we don't know. However often we go for ultrasounds, however much we submit to prenatal testing to learn about the gender and size and health of our soon-to-be offspring, even those who embark upon parenting in the most considered and controlled and rational way possible *do not know who is coming.* Having a child is, arguably, the deepest and most enduring connection of which we are capable, and we don't know who it is we are proposing to devote our work and worry to for the next eighteen or twenty years. This has to be the ultimate blind date! Only it is more like an arranged marriage, for when this stranger arrives you are not just courting: you are already committed. If it were not so commonplace, we would think it was madness.

Here is a social arrangement in which rational, self-sufficient actors, perfectly capable of judging their own best interests and maximizing them, commit themselves sight unseen to a being who will reliably cost them enormous time, money, labor, anxiety, and grief for a mixed and unreliable long-range return. Sometimes we do it by conscious choice, carefully timing a pregnancy to fit in with other life activities. Often enough we do it by accident or by default, or for reasons that may be good or bad or foolish. But however it comes about, with an amazing degree of regularity, we accept our children as they come to us, receive them for no other reason than that they somehow belong to us and we to them, and we do our best through the years that follow to figure out what is good for them and provide it as well as we can.

Of course, we do not merely passively receive our children, but also actively shape who they will become, socializing and educating them, forming and directing their development according to our own judgments and convictions. Along with devotion to our children in the present go plans and dreams about their future, and all the goods we hope to see realized in their lives. But no one with any real involvement in the upbringing of a child could subscribe to philosopher John Locke's theory that a child is a blank tablet upon which anything at all can be written. Children from birth both absorb and resist our influence, bringing to the equation their own inclinations and abilities, their own preferences and limitations, their own nature, and, very soon, their own choices about who they wish to become. The actual experience of parenting is always an interplay between planning and happenstance, between the weighty sense of responsibility and the frustration of helplessness. Experienced parents know they cannot, and wise parents know they should not, undertake to impose their own version of the ideal child upon their offspring. And they also know something of the grief that goes with accepting all the things they care passionately about but cannot control.

Despite its many discomforts, pregnancy is a perennial wonder.

What all this underscores is the complexity and delicacy of the moral task that parents undertake, to be thoroughly interested and invested participants in the nurture of another human being who will in the end meet them as an equal, and will certainly not always please them. Parenting is the risky enterprise in which one merely human being sets out to form another, and it requires a whole panoply of virtues: flexibility and courage and humility, humor and restraint and above all a deep generosity of spirit. For here human beings are asked to use an enormous disparity of power unselfishly and with a deliberate intent to see it overturned in the end in favor of the liberty and responsibility of one who stands in primary relation to God. We discover our children's good rather than determine it, and in the end we will complete our duties to our children by stepping back from their lives as they become in actuality what they have always been in origin and in destiny: our peers and not our subjects, fellow creatures with us and "coheirs of the grace of life."

Cloning as a technique of selection

On this specifically theological note I want to pause, to propose that we think about what difference it will make to us and to our children if we move from this basic stance of receiving and welcoming and cherishing the children who are born to us to one of selecting them, or more properly selecting in advance a template that is to be reproduced in them. What will it mean to our understanding of our offspring and our relation to them if they are not gifts who surprise us but projects we have engineered, whose most basic biological attributes are the product of our will? What will it do to parenting if we go to such lengths as asexual replication in order to exercise control over every element of the individual genome?

One of the things such a practice will do is to place parental desires, not simply the general desire to have a baby but the desire for a *particular* baby, squarely in the center of what constitutes the parent-child relationship. We will have moved from the experience at once routine and extraordinary of being presented with a child who is one's to nurture and to celebrate, to the quite different experience of the delivery of a specific and intended result, inevitably measured against the prototype chosen for replication. It is not hard to see why so many fear that our attitude about this relationship among both technicians and prospective parents will shift toward child-as-commodity afforded to parent-as-consumer. The traditional language of Christians and Jews, that children are gifts of God, can only seem quaint and out of place in a context in which people can speak without blushing of "quality control."

On the other hand, what cloning will not do is successfully eliminate uncertainty. Some of the rationales proposed for human cloning reflect not only an unseemly desire to control who our offspring will be but also a great lack of sophistication in understanding human development. Any behavioral scientist can tell you that a person is far too complex an interaction of genotype, physical environment, social context, and individual life experience to be engineered reliably. The odds are overwhelming that you cannot make yourself another Michael Jordan or another Yo-Yo Ma, or even another you, even if it were morally legitimate to set out to do so. But the fact that it will not work is little comfort, for what would it be like to live as a failed copy or to be the parent of one? Successful or not, our readiness to engineer the genome of our offspring to obtain a desirable result expresses a lack of fundamental respect for the otherness of our children, who not only are not us but are finally not ours.

It is not hard to see why so many fear that our attitude about this relationship. . . . will shift toward child-as-commodity afforded to parent-as-consumer.

In my judgment, human reproductive cloning as a technique of genetic engineering represents a basic distortion of parenting. It displays a failure of the reticence rooted in religious awe with which people of faith should approach intervention in the being of another human creature. This reticence is most important precisely where it is most in danger of subversion, in the intense and emotion-laden relationship between parent and child, where such enormous influence is exerted and such disparate power is exercised. By making our offspring the product not of our bodies and our relationships but of our will, we give a new and peculiarly intimate form to a most fundamental human corruption: the readiness to make ourselves each the center of our own universe and to regard all others in relation to ourselves.

Cloning as a remedy for deprivation

Now finally I come around to the arguments for reproductive cloning as a means of providing a child under special circumstances that rule out other methods. Rationales have included the desire to produce a child who is genetically related to a sterile donor, as in Tendler's example; the wish to replace a dead fetus or child in cases like that proposed by Cole-Turner; and the possibility of providing a genetically related child to a lesbian couple, in Lebacqz's discussion. I will not pretend that such circumstances do not represent real losses, even in some cases real tragedies. But I question whether it is always possible to offer a technical solution to a human reality such as sterility or premature death, and whether it is always desirable to do so simply because it is possible. Such questions are always subject to the charge of heartlessness, especially when they are raised by people who do not confront in their own lives the realities with which these proposals try to grapple. Nevertheless, I think we are in danger of serious distortions of life and thought if we do not think long and hard about what we are trying to do with biomedical technology and why, and if we don't stop to consider who we turn ourselves and each other into along the way. Taking these examples as instances of a larger class of exceptional cases, I will treat them in the order given. My aim is to achieve some clarity about what possibilities cloning would or would not offer in such cases.

As human beings, our task is not to outwit death, but to become people who can live mortal lives.

Rabbi Tendler's scenario proposes to use cloning to continue a family line for a sterile man whose relatives have all died in the Holocaust. He speaks of a religious and cultural value placed on familial continuity, and of the peculiar horror of the Nazi genocide as destroying whole families, root and branch. These are matters of enormous weight and seriousness, not to be passed off lightly. What the world has lost in the destruction of so much of European Jewry is incalculable, as indeed are the losses of every such slaughter, both those known and those buried in the silence of history. But it is important to be clear about what cloning can and cannot offer here. It cannot restore either the children who were or the children who would have been, not as individuals and not as collective carriers of all the particular genetic mix that might be thought to underlie a "family line." It cannot even give the hypothetical man a child in the normal sense of the word, a descendant half of whose genetic complement comes from the father without replicating any of his genome. It can only give the sterile man a delayed genetic twin, a child who, far from rescuing familial continuity, is not exactly anyone's son or daughter. The idea that this is the only or the best way to resist the destruction of a family strikes me as wrongheaded, as if the transmission of DNA decisively constituted human identity and belonging, and gave meaning to what we express when we call our families "ours." It seems to me that Rabbi Tendler's hypothetical survivor would be better served by adopting a child and raising her or him in the history and the traditions, the memories and the love that are the real stuff of family life and continuity.

The case envisioned by Cole-Turner is at once more poignant and more troubling. It presents us with a grief more imaginable and distinct: the loss of a child late in pregnancy by a couple who can conceive no more. There is no issue here of genetic replication of parent or living donor, and no actual developed human being who would have been selected in the person of the clone. What there is instead is a chance to cheat death by cloning the fetus from salvaged tissue, and thus to replace for the couple what, one might argue, nature and even God intended: a living child born of their union. It seems we have here the opportunity to provide a technical fix for tragedy. But do we? Even if we do, is it one we ought to use?

A dead child can't be returned

The reality is that such a couple has experienced a real loss, an actual death, and that fact must not be denied or minimized lest it come back to haunt both the parents and any child to be born. Neither by cloning nor by any other technique is it possible to give back the dead child; the question is whether we ought to try to give the grieving parents a twin to replace it. In more ordinary circumstances, parents experiencing such a late-term loss would be counseled to take time to live with and come to terms with their grief before making an effort to conceive a "new" baby, precisely because of the moral and psychological problems inherent in trying to replace one human being with another. Such concerns could only be dramatically heightened if the new fetus were a clone of the child now dead. As harsh as it may seem, I am convinced that this utterly understandable impulse is a temptation we should resist. Rather than finding a technical circumvention of mortality, we must find the courage to face it squarely, to endure the suffering it imposes, and to move toward the recovery of faith and hope through grief rather than around it. As human beings, our task is not to outwit death, but to become people who can live mortal lives, loving other mortals wisely and well. Since the natural conception of another child is (hypothetically) impossible, the alternatives for such a couple would be other means of assisted reproduction (the specific means would depend on the nature of the infertility, now unspecified), or the adoption of a child who would be their second child, not a recreation of the first; a child made theirs by love and the thousand shared tasks of parenting, rather than by genetic relationship.

Finally, I turn to the question of whether cloning should be used to extend the right to a child related to them and no one else to couples who in the nature of the case cannot conceive one in the ordinary fashion: lesbian couples. Here I want to affirm Lebacqz's insight that to pose the question in this way reveals how far, and how far astray, we have come in our pursuit of technological reproduction. In our urgency to provide would-be parents with whatever they want, and can pay for, we have allowed ourselves to forget a lesson that should have been burned into our brains with the abolition of slavery and the repeal of laws that made women and children property: no one can have a right to another human being.

In our lives as members of families, however constituted, we are gifted with one another rather than entitled to one another. . . . Our children are ours, or perhaps more deeply we are theirs, because we receive and welcome them, because we put ourselves in service to them, and finally because we understand both the depth and the limits of human belonging. Our insistence on "children of our own" and our readiness to go to any expense, any risk, any length to obtain offspring who carry our genes and no one else's, reveal not so much our prizing of family as our misunderstanding of it.

7

Cloning Harms Animals

Andrew Breslin

Andrew Breslin is outreach coordinator of the American Anti-Vivisection Society.

Cloning will lead to the abuse of animals by animal researchers and the agricultural industry. Scientists will clone genetically identical animals for use in unscientific and cruel animal experiments. Moreover, scientists working for the agriculture industry will clone animals that produce more milk and meat simply to improve profits.

Dolly, the sheep who is the first clone produced from cells taken from an adult mammal has set off controversy throughout the world, but most of the discussion has centered around the implications of human cloning. There has been a conspicuous absence in the public debate regarding the fundamental change in the relationships between human beings and the rest of nature which has come, and is continuing to unfold, as a result of the new biotechnology.

Animal exploitation

The introduction of cloning will open new avenues of animal exploitation and will streamline some old ones. Dolly was "created" in the interests of a company which seeks to develop animals as "bioreactors." Cloning is also likely to lead to the mass production of transgenic animals of all kinds, including animals designed for xenotransplantation, if that frightening practice is not halted. Altering DNA is a tricky, often hit-or-miss business. Now animals successfully "created" with altered DNA will be copied many times, as if they were mere documents and not living beings.

It is probable that even "normal" animals used in laboratories will be cloned in the near future. In the quest to eliminate every variable other than the obvious one of the differences between the animals under study and the human recipients of the therapies which may one day result, scientists will soon have legions of genetically identical animals upon whom to perform experiments. Ironically, the humans who will one day receive the resulting medications are likely to remain as genetically diverse as ever, making experiments on homogenous animals even further removed from the reality of human medicine.

Although animal experimentation is an enormous industry, it is eclipsed by the animal agriculture industry. The number of animals who suffer and die to satisfy humans' unnatural eating habits is many times that of those who suffer in laboratories—in fact, for all other human purposes combined. Therefore, in sheer numbers, cloning is likely to have its most dramatic impact on the animal victims of this industry.

The animal industries have ignored the ethical implications of the new technologies, apparently seeing nothing but dollar signs.

The large-scale factory farming of animals is evidence of our arrogance as a species, treating other animals as nothing more than machinery. Now we are redesigning the "machines" themselves for no other purpose than to increase the economic returns of the industry.

For decades, animal agriculture industries have pursued biotechnology as a means of increasing profits. At a recent conference on the genetic modification of "livestock," representatives of these industries listened excitedly to presentation by Ian Wilmut, one of Dolly's "creators."

The successful cloning from a cell of an adult mammal has encouraged the animal agriculture industries, who eagerly look forward to knocking out or adding specific genes to produce more profitable animals. In the past, such attempts at manipulation produced nothing but additional suffering. For example, the genetic manipulation of pigs to make them leaner resulted in animals which developed ulcers, lameness, and other physical problems. Selective breeding, a slower form of our genetic control of animals has also resulted in severe physical problems for animals.

Ethical implications

Not surprisingly, the animal industries have ignored the ethical implications of the new technologies, apparently seeing nothing but dollar signs, and considering any deeper appraisal a nuisance. This statement by Gary Webber of the National Cattleman's and Beef Association typifies this myopic viewpoint: "I see more and more consumer pressure for 'natural approaches' to production." The furor over cloning, he said, reveals "a widening gap between science and public understanding. I think we are going to have people screaming, 'stop this train for a while,' while society confronts the ethical and health issues of animal modification."

The context of Mr. Webber's statement makes it clear that he feels that confronting ethical and health issues is something he'd prefer we not do.

It is particularly disturbing to see the intense debate over the bioethical issues concerning cloning human beings but little discussion of what it means to manipulate the very structure of other species to serve as meat and milk machines. Dolly symbolizes everything that is wrong with our relationship with other animals, not only born to serve misguided human desires, but actually designed for no other purpose. In a display of extreme and sad irony, Ian Wilmut received a package from some well-meaning Canadian school children: It was filled with birthday cards for Dolly.

8

Cloning Can Help Humans and Animals

Ian Wilmut, Keith Campbell, and Colin Tudge

Ian Wilmut, an embryologist, led the team of scientists that cloned Dolly at the Roslin Institute in Edinburgh, Scotland. Keith Campbell, a cell biologist and embryologist, worked with Wilmut on the project that resulted in Dolly. Colin Tudge is a science writer who is also a Research Fellow at the Centre for Philosophy at the London School of Economics.

Scientists can use cloning to produce more suitable laboratory animals, more productive dairy cows, and to reproduce endangered species. Cloning avoids the problems associated with inbreeding, which frequently results in offspring plagued by genetic disorders.

Tomorrow's biology, swollen with the new techniques and insights that will accrue from the science and technologies of cloning, now promises us a measure of control over life's processes that in practice will seem absolute. It would be dangerous ever to suppose that we can understand all of life's processes exhaustively: this would lead us into the Greek sin of hubris, with all the penalties that follow. Yet our descendants will find themselves with power that seems limited only by their imagination—that, plus the laws of physics and the rules of logic.

Prediction is a dangerous game, but it is one we should never stop trying to play. So let us look at what seems feasible in the light of current knowledge. . . .

Cloning for the laboratory

Cloning laboratory animals may seem too obvious to be worth comment, but there is more to it than meets the eye. The central aim, of course, is to produce animals for experimentation that are genetically uniform, so that when scientists try out a particular drug or training method or other procedure, they know that any differences they perceive are due to the procedure and not to genetic differences between the animals. But there are various difficulties. Notably, the traditional way—and up to now the only way—to produce genetically uniform strains of, say, mice has been by inbreeding. Closely related individuals are mated, and their offspring are remated, until a population is produced that is all of a muchness.

But as everyone knows, such inbreeding is dangerous. It is for this reason that various genetic disorders, including porphyria and hemophilia, have bedeviled various royal houses in Europe. The problem lies with excess *homozygosity*. Every individual inherits one set of genes from one parent, and another set from the other parent. If the two parents are not closely related, then the two sets of genes will differ somewhat. You might, for example, inherit a gene for red hair from your mother, and a gene for dark hair from your father. Then you are said to be *heterozygous* for that particular gene for hair color. But if you inherited a gene for red hair from both parents, you would be homozygous for that hair color gene. The trouble begins when one of the genes in a matching pair is a deleterious mutant—for example, the one that produces cystic fibrosis. If you inherit a cystic fibrosis mutant from one parent and a normal gene from the other, then you will not suffer from the disease; your heterozygosity saves you. But if you inherit the CF gene from both parents, you will be affected. Of course, only a minority of genes are as harmful as the CF mutant, but the principle applies broadly, and too much homozygosity leads to the general loss of fitness known as inbreeding depression.

It would sometimes be good to work with creatures that are more "natural.". . . Cloning helps here.

So if you produce laboratory animals simply by inbreeding, then you will perforce produce a great deal of homozygosity, which is likely to lead to inbreeding depression. In fact *most* attempts to produce purebred strains of laboratory mice have failed. The strains that exist today are the minority that have survived inbreeding, fortunate beasts that happen, by chance, to lack a significant number of genes that are deleterious so that they avoid the kinds of effects we see in cystic fibrosis. We have to conclude, though, that laboratory mice are genetically peculiar because most animals simply cannot withstand such a high degree of homozygosity. Yet it happens, too, that inbreeding does not produce quite such uniformity as might be supposed. Sometimes there has proved to be a remarkable amount of genetic variation (implying heterozygosity) in laboratory strains that are supposed to be completely uniform.

On the other hand, it would sometimes be good to work with creatures that are more "natural": that is, are more heterozygous. Cloning helps here, as well. It not only offers a route to complete genetic uniformity—at least of the nuclear genes—but also makes it possible to produce strains that are uniform but *not* homozygous. In fact, a highly heterozygous wild mouse—or in principle a wild anything—could be cloned to produce as many genetic facsimiles as required. We are so used to thinking that genetic uniformity can be produced only by inbreeding that we tend to assume that uniformity must imply homozygosity. But consider, say, any one variety of domestic potato. Any particular King Edward or Maris Piper might well be highly heterozygous, but since it is multiplied by cloning (via tubers), each individual potato is genetically similar to all the others, and so the variety as a whole is uniform.

The advantages that may accrue from producing genetically identical laboratory animal strains *without* inbreeding could, as the decades pass, prove very helpful.

Replicating the elite

Similar considerations—and more—apply to the cloning of farm livestock. On the one hand, farmers seek uniformity: they want to know how their animals are liable to perform under particular conditions, when they are liable to mature, and so on; and so, of course, do their markets. On the other hand, farmers also seek optimum performance, where "optimum" does not necessarily mean "maximum," although increasingly this is the case. Among, say, dairy cattle there is a huge difference between the yield of the milkiest cows, commonly called elite animals, and of the least endowed. A wild cow produces around 300 gallons of milk in a year to feed her solitary calf, while many modern Friesians produce 2,000 gallons and more. Of course, a modern farmer would have a herd of purebred Friesians, but even in one elite herd, there is commonly a twofold difference between the milkiest animals (2,000 gallons) and the average (around 1,000 gallons). In general, farmers seek to bring the average up to the level of the best. But such "improvements" (this is the technical term) take a very long time. The farmer normally improves his herd by impregnating his better cows by AI with semen from an elite bull. But only half the calves produced will be female, and each of them takes three years from conception to first lactation (a working year for her own gestation, then a year to mature, then another nine months to produce a calf as a prelude to lactation). In short, raising the standard of a herd even when the farmer has access to the world's best bulls is a slow business. In breeding time, the average animals are commonly considered to be ten years behind the elite.

Cloning could also be of immense, perhaps even critical, value in animal conservation.

There are further complications. Just as animals (and plants) suffer from inbreeding depression when they are too homozygous, they can also experience what Charles Darwin called hybrid vigor when they are outbred and thus highly heterozygous. Farmers of animals, like growers of potatoes, would in general like to combine overall uniformity with individual heterozygosity. In addition, farmers often seek to combine the qualities of different breeds, so that dairy farmers commonly cross Friesian dairy cows with beefy bulls (such as Herefords or Charolais) to produce calves that are good for beef (since only a minority of calves born in a dairy herd are needed as herd replacements). Among sheep farmers, juggling the options between uplands and lowlands, the crossing permutations can be quite bewildering.

In all such instances where the need is to raise herd quality quickly, and/or to combine uniformity with heterozygosity, cloning has an obvious role. A dairy farmer might improve his herd significantly in ten years by purchasing sperm from an elite bull, but he might achieve the same improvement in one season by furnishing his cows with ready-made embryos that have been cloned from some elite animal. No wonder the Americans invested so much in this technology in the 1980s. Of course, ultrahigh performance does raise special issues of animal welfare—which alone must set limits on what can be done. On the other hand, cloning and embryo transfer could be of particular value in the Third World, where cattle are vital to the economy, where they are often multipurpose (cows might be required to pull carts as well as to provide calves and milk, though they may feed mainly on straw and must withstand tropical heat), and where breeding is particularly difficult because of the many contrasting qualities that are required in any one animal. Whether the economic "incentives" exist to take the new technologies into poor countries is another question.

Cloning for conservation

Cloning could also be of immense, perhaps even critical, value in animal conservation. Many have doubted this. The critics point out, for example, that the task for conservationists is to maintain the maximum possible genetic diversity within each breeding population and point out, rightly, that cloning does not increase diversity. It merely replicates what is there already. This is precisely the point. Conservationists cannot *add* to the range of genes that currently exists. But they must strive to minimize the rate at which genetic diversity is lost. The great enemy is "genetic drift," the steady loss of genetic variation, generation by generation. When animals breed, each parent passes on only *half* of his or her genes to each offspring. If the animal has hundreds or millions of offspring, like a fly or a codfish, then there is a very good chance that each parent will indeed pass on all of its genes, which will be spread randomly among the many offspring. But an animal like a rhinoceros or an orangutan may have only about half a dozen offspring in a lifetime, so some of its genes are liable to remain uninherited. If the population of rhinos or orangs is large, then any one variant of any one gene is liable to be contained within many different individuals, so the breeding animals should pass on all the genes in the total gene pool. But if the breeding population is low—as it is bound to be if the animal is already rare—then the less common genes may well be contained within only one or a few individuals, and the individual containing the rarest genes may well finish its reproductive life without passing them on. Hence generational loss of variation.

Conservation biologists attempt to minimize loss by genetic drift by complicated breeding schemes intended to ensure that each individual that can breed does indeed mate (while avoiding inbreeding), but these schemes are expensive and difficult to organize. Yet it would be technically easy to take tissue samples (biopsies) from representative members of all the endangered species of mammals that now exist (about 200 at least are priorities), culture them, and then put the cultures in deep freeze. (If the biopsies were simply frozen without culturing them first, they would probably be damaged. Cultures are two-dimensional—one cell layer thick—while biopsies are three-dimensional blocks of tissue; it is hard to freeze a block uniformly.) If the samples were well chosen, they could contain virtually all the genes now present in existing species. In fifty years' time, when the technology that produced Dolly is well advanced and can be extended readily to other species, and when the species that are now endangered are on their last legs and have lost much of their present variation through genetic drift, cells from those frozen cell cultures could be made into Dolly-style embryos, and future creatures could give birth to offspring as diverse as those of today. Since the present-day breeding schemes are so difficult to run and organize (among other things, they require cooperation among people who tend to be highly individualistic), the Dolly technology could offer the most realistic option for many of our best-loved and ecologically most significant wild creatures.

9

A Personal Defense of Human Cloning

Jonathan Colvin

Jonathan Colvin is a freelance technical writer who lives in Vancouver, British Columbia, Canada.

The overwhelming majority of objections to human cloning seem to be grounded in cheap science fiction movies such as *Frankenstein*. Yet many overlook the fact that earlier reproductive technologies such as "test tube" babies, which were vehemently criticized, are now widely accepted and even applauded. Moreover, few condemn natural clones—that is, identical twins. The author suffers from cystic fibrosis, an inherited genetic condition. Because of his affliction, he cannot have children. It is his dream to clone himself and repair the genetic defect that the clone will unquestionably inherit from him. In that way he will be giving his clone the opportunity which fate stole from him—the ability to have children and the possibility of enjoying a long life.

Clone. To many people the word has sinister overtones; it's a disturbing amalgam of flesh and technology. A poll revealed that 88 percent of Canadians believe that human cloning should be illegal, and most governments are moving to concur.

Interested in this near-unanimous sentiment, I carried out my own impromptu survey of friends and strangers. Most said they agreed with the prohibition of human cloning. But when I asked them to explain exactly why they thought it should be illegal, the poll became much more revealing.

Many mumbled about the dangers of "cloning Hitler" or creating a subclass of slaves. Others brought up the specter of basketball teams full of identical seven-foot-tall players. A smaller, more thoughtful percentage believed it would be unnatural or the ultimate in narcissism. In general, however, public attitudes toward human cloning seem to be based on a diet of science-fiction B-movies and paperbacks.

But should human cloning be feared, as the next Frankenstein's monster of genetic engineering?

While undoubtedly fascinating, few people would perceive identical twins to be the least bit sinister. And yet identical twins are in fact natural clones, formed from the same egg and sharing the same genotype. If natural clones are not to be feared, why should we fear the deliberate ones?

With the coming genetic revolution, we will be directing our own evolution rather than relying on a natural . . . lottery to do it for us.

Many of the attitudes concerning human cloning are reminiscent of the arguments against in vitro fertilization in the 1960s, when accusations of "playing God" and interfering with nature were common. Today, however, "test tube" babies are celebrated for their own individuality and as people in their own right. Exactly, say opponents of cloning. Babies born in vitro are unique individuals; clones are photocopies of people who already exist. What will happen to individuality if we can stamp out copies of ourselves like so many cookies on a tray?

Interestingly, many of those who make this argument also tend to emphasize nurture over nature and deny that our genes determine ourselves— whether it be IQ, athletic ability, or our favorite ice cream flavor. But these arguments contradict each other. For if nurture triumphs over nature, then a clone will be an individual as unique as any other, determined for the most part by the environment in which she or he was reared.

Perhaps the most weighty argument against cloning is that, by eliminating the mixing of genes that occurs during conventional reproduction, human biodiversity will be diminished and human evolution will cease. It is the serendipitous mixing of genes that produces the Einsteins and Mozarts of the world; take away this process and surely the potential for new genius will cease. However, the fact is that human biological evolution for all intents and purposes has become insignificant compared to cultural evolution.

"I wish to clone myself"

At this point, it is appropriate that I reveal the source of my interest in this subject. For the truth is, I wish to clone myself. Before my gate is stormed by villagers wielding branding irons, let me explain why.

I am thirty-two years old and have cystic fibrosis, an inherited genetic disease that prohibits those who suffer from it from conceiving children and usually kills by the mid-thirties. My dream is to clone myself, repair my clone's genetic defect, and give him the opportunity to fulfill the potential that has been denied to me by a cruel quirk of nature.

Perhaps my clone will climb Mount Everest, singlehandedly sail around the world, or simply marry and raise a family without the fear that his children will be prematurely fatherless and his wife a widow. The clone will not be me, but perhaps he will be who I could have been.

My body, my self. Surely also my DNA, my self.

With the coming genetic revolution, we will be directing our own evolution rather than relying on a natural (and sometimes disastrous) lottery to do it for us. And surely cloning will remain an esoteric and unusual method of reproduction, with most people choosing to do it the old-fashioned (and far more pleasurable) way. But should government be able to tell me what I can or cannot do with what is, after all, an intrinsic part of what and who I am?

Criminalizing an activity may be easier than answering the thorny philosophical questions raised by it. But before government rushes to outlaw my dream, it should at least seriously consider whether the opposition to human cloning is based on real dangers.

10

Religion Should Not Influence Public Policy on Cloning

Gregory E. Pence

Gregory E. Pence is professor of philosophy in the schools of Medicine and Arts/Humanities at the University of Alabama, Birmingham, where he has taught and written about bioethics for over twenty years. He is the author of Classic Cases in Medical Ethics, *editor of* Classic Works in Medical Ethics, *and co-author of* Seven Dilemmas in World Religion.

The most general argument against cloning by theologians is that it violates God's will. Religious opponents cite scriptures, especially the story of creation in Genesis to illustrate their objection. However, scriptures are merely ancient tales with no literal basis in reality. It would, therefore, be a serious error to base public policy upon ancient folklore. Moreover, it would violate the constitutional ban on the separation of church and state.

The most general argument against creating an adult human being by NST [Nuclear Somatic Transfer] is that it is against the will of God. Some people believe that humans have no right to change the way that humans are created because sexual reproduction was ordained by God and that to try to change this way is sinful.

Upon hearing the news of Dolly [the cloned sheep], Duke University divinity professor Stanley Hauerwas said that those who wanted to clone Dolly "are going to try to sell it with wonderful benefits" to medical and animal industries. He condemned the procedure because he thought it was "a kind of drive behind this for us to be our own creators," raising the images of Dr. Frankenstein and human hubris. A scant ten days after Dolly's announcement, the Christian Life Commission of the Southern Baptist Convention predictably called for a federal law against human cloning, as well as an international law to the same effect. The Vatican in April of 1997 asserted: "the right to be born in a human way." It urged all nations to ban human cloning and, in manner typical of Vatican ethics, urged them to make no exceptions. An enlightened Shi'ite Muslim jurist named Sheikh Fadlallah suggested that originating a child by cloning should be punished by death or, at the very least, amputation.

The NBAC [National Bioethics Advisory Commission] *Report* quoted Paul Ramsey's dictum that, "Religious people have never denied, indeed they affirm, that God means to kill us all in the end, and in the end he is going to succeed." As said, testifying before NBAC, Lutheran theologian Gilbert Meilaender emphasized the importance of "the creation story in the first chapter of Genesis [that] depicts the creation of humankind as male and female, sexually differentiated and enjoined by God's grace to sustain human life through procreation." Other theologians testifying emphasized the Scriptural basis of: God's creation of humans, warnings not to play God, dangers of the quest for knowledge, the need for responsible dominion over nature, and the ultimate folly of human destiny.

In the image of God

Verses 26–27 of the first chapter of Genesis tell us, "And God said, Let us make man in our image, after our likeness . . . So God created man in his own image, in the image of God created he them; male and female created he them." Two chapters later, we get another famous, relevant story:

> 6 And when the woman saw that the tree was good for food, and that it was pleasant to the eyes, and a tree to be desired to make one wise, she took of the fruit thereof, and did eat, and gave also unto her husband with her; and he did eat.

> 7 And the eyes of them both were opened, and they knew that they were naked; and they sewed fig leaves together, and made themselves aprons.

This story tells an oft-told tale in the Old Testament that once-upon-a-time there was a time of moral perfection, but because of some bad act of humans, things changed and disaster followed. Genesis describes Eden as a pure and simple land that ultimately gets so corrupted that God brings the great flood, allowing only Noah and his family to escape. Often the agent of corruption is the human quest for knowledge, represented by the Tower of Babel, which also signifies human hubris before God.

Many of the events described in Genesis, especially the story of the Garden of Eden, are not actual events but symbolic fables.

These stories are our most ancient tales and, as such, resonate deeply within us. They convey the message that a small bit of new knowledge can be treacherous for humanity. Humanity is forbidden from knowing certain things, and the consequence of knowing these things is that a black cloak of doom will cover our world.

Despite these deeply-ingrained feelings, it is a grave mistake to let such ancient stories dictate modern public policy. First, and most obviously, they are just stories. Many of the events described in Genesis, especially the story of the Garden of Eden, are not actual events but symbolic fables, repeated in many Near Eastern cultures. For example, pre-Hebraic civilizations such as Babylonia also had the story of a great flood.

Second, and of equal importance, the Old Testament is not full of moral wisdom. Although Meilaender's entire testimony derives from these Scriptural stories, like all such references to Scripture, he only goes there to justify what he already believes. If a neutral person merely read the Old Testament and followed what it said, he would find that: Abraham and King David make women captured in war into slaves in their harems; Exodus 21:2 condones human slavery; Jephthah's daughter is required as a human sacrifice; sex with slave-maids is permitted to create male heirs when Sarah's and Rachel's husbands are barren; and Exodus 23:27 permits killing women and children of enemies in war.

The U.S. Constitution forbids the establishment of laws and policies that are solely motivated by religious beliefs.

Genesis 3:16 also says famously, "Unto the woman he said, I will greatly multiply thy sorrow and thy conception; in sorrow thou shalt bring forth children; and thy desire shall be to thy husband, and he shall rule over thee." Obviously, this event could not have really happened and must just be a story, because otherwise we are forced to see God as utterly unjust. Not only is Eve punished for her own act, so are billions of women afterwards in human history who must experience painful childbirth. Although Scripture condones these injustices, Meilaender undoubtedly does not think them right, and that is because he has some non-Scriptural standard of right on which to base his judgment. It is also worth noting that rabbis such as Moses Tendler, who also testified before NBAC and whose religion has been studying Genesis longer than Christianity, do not think that the creation story of Genesis implies an absolute ban on human cloning.

Consider also that the story of the Tree of Knowledge is about moral knowledge: "then your eyes shall be opened, and ye shall be as gods, knowing good and evil" (3:5). What should we infer from this story. That humans should know nothing about morality? Perhaps humans made no moral judgments in the Garden of Eden, but how is that story relevant to a world where humans must constantly do so?

A fatalistic worldview

To accept Old Testament morality in general is to accept a fatalistic worldview. That is understandable because the Old Testament was edited to its final form over two thousand years ago when being fatalistic made sense. The Old Testament did not anticipate genetic therapy, artificial skin, and organ transplants.

In more modern theology, it takes a mighty lot of intermediate steps of interpretation and reasoning to get from (1) A rational God exists and cares about us, to (2) It is immoral to originate a human by NST. Such steps would have to counter the premises that, (3) Because a rational God exists and cares about us, He allows us to make new discoveries in medicine and science, and that, (4) Because God is rational and cares about us, he directs us to create humans in ways that are rational and that express caring about human beings. Substantial argument would be needed to prove that originating a child by NST by parents with good motives was against (4). I do not think that can be done.

After all the dust settles about originating babies by NST, it may turn out that opposition to it stems *only* from religious people or from those whose thinking is colored by traditional religious beliefs. If so, isn't there a problem with recognizing such views in American law? The U.S. Constitution forbids the establishment of laws and policies that are solely motivated by religious beliefs. Should studies in non-human mammalian embryogenesis indicate that NST would be safe in humans, and should well-motivated parents be identified who had good reasons to try it (being at risk for having babies with genetic disease), would not further opposition be solely based on religious grounds? And as such, would it not violate our Constitution to have it ground a federal ban that restricts others' reproductive freedom?

lation and about relatedness itself is programmed in and received through the genes of parents. People get married, make babies, and raise them in ways that seem normal to us because of our history, the habits passed down through the last three or four generations of Western families. It is only recently that we could consider the possibility of lesbian or gay reproduction, or ponder the relative value of different kinds of offspring or relatedness. So our efforts to squeeze every case into a standard of deviation from the normal model of birds and bees is merely a kind of collective dissonance with forming new habits about such an intimate matter. Moreover, we struggle in our new technologies to restore the apparent equilibrium of the "classical" family, work to find technologies that give us as much of the birds and bees as is possible. This is one reason why, for example, most couples will use sperm injection rather than donor sperm. It is simply assumed that it is better, more normal, to have a child that shares more identity with me. Thinking about and emphasizing the role of children's stories helps to bring these two issues into focus.

The family is . . . only one among many institutions that raises children.

But our habits in making our own families are only part of the culture of reproduction. Parenthood is for some purposes at the luxury of the community, and it is more than idle Platonic fantasy that children are raised by the state. . . . Economics, politics, and theology play roles in how infertility is understood and treated. The family is also only one among many institutions that raises children. In fact, when parents fail in a variety of tasks (from immunization to feeding to education), they can lose their parental rights, to be restored only at the discretion of representatives of our democracy. The upstream manifestation of this public concern for the welfare of children is manifest when, for example, it is argued that children in general ought not be born clones, or that research to clone humans is of a comparatively low priority in the existing array of choices for research spending. Even editors of scientific journals and newspapers have a choice about what they will send out for review and in what way they will publish findings about cloning. The goal of examining culture is to square the variety of contexts within which a tool comes to be with the ends it is actually capable of achieving. John Dewey calls this the placing of means and ends in strict conjunction and points to the continuum between means and ends for the purpose of seeing our social methods solve social problems.

Common sense and cloning

Common sense is the most misunderstood element of practical ethics. The idea is not to skip the difficult questions and move on to easy progress. As is already apparent, in the present case we want to unpack the meaning of satisfying the complex and situated demands of a variety of people within a social context. More, ethical evaluation of social problems requires that one take seriously the challenges of science to social

thought, and in this respect cloning is clearly a paradigm case. Cloning does not uniquely challenge what it is to make a child, but it has called attention to the vast array of new technologies that make new kinds of families whose parameters and relationships are neither pregiven nor socially sanctioned. It is insufficient to ask, as do most critics of cloning, whether a child of cloning would be deprived of a right to individuality. No child has an open future, and even a cursory examination of the changing history of parenthood makes clear that it is not individuality but rather correct forms of responsible relation that is the goal.

I have not addressed . . . the tough or exceptional cases. . . . The tough cases are interesting. . . . But the pragmatic question is more interesting: What institutions and arenas are right for situating the debate about human cloning? . . . I have argued that the adoption procedure is a metaphor for what is possible: regional, localized evaluation of candidates for new procedures, accompanied by education and tolerance of new kinds of families and reproduction. But other and more experimental methods too may be called for. We have begun to reconstruct the entire enterprise of making children in the twenty-first century as a backdrop for debate about human cloning. Once this is accomplished, we can move beyond exceptional approaches to general problems and develop new institutional and personal habits for making and supporting families in the twenty-first century.

12

There Is Nothing Inherently Wrong with Human Cloning

Richard Dawkins

Richard Dawkins is the Charles Simonyi Professor of Public Understanding of Science at Oxford University.

When the cloning of Dolly the sheep first became public, an overwhelming majority of people responded to the procedure negatively. Moreover, the prospect of cloning humans was greeted with universal repugnance. Simply put, however, cloning is not the science fiction nightmare portrayed by its detractors. In fact, cloning is a more natural procedure than sexual reproduction. In any case, the burden of proof resides with those who would ban human cloning, not with those who support it.

Science and logic cannot tell us what is right and what is wrong. You cannot, as I was once challenged to do by a belligerent radio interviewer, prove logically from scientific evidence that murder is wrong. But you can deploy logical reasoning, and even scientific facts, in demonstrating to dogmatists that their convictions are mutually contradictory. You can prove that their passionate denunciation of X is incompatible with their equally passionate advocacy of Y, because X and Y, though they had not realized it before, are the same thing. Science can show us a new way of thinking about an issue, perhaps open our imaginations in unexpected ways, with the consequence that we see our personal Xs and Ys in different ways and our values change. Sometimes we can be shown a way of seeing that makes us feel more favorably disposed to something that had been distasteful or frightening. But we can also be alerted to menacing implications of something that we had previously thought harmless or frivolously amusing. Cloning provides a case study in the power of scientific thinking to change our minds, in both directions.

Public responses to Dolly the sheep varied but there was almost universal agreement that such a thing must never be allowed to happen to

From "What's Wrong with Cloning?" by Richard Dawkins, *Clones and Cloning: Facts and Fantasies About Human Cloning,* edited by Martha C. Nussbaum and Cass R. Sunsteins (New York: W.W. Norton & Company, 1998). Copyright © 1998 by W.W. Norton & Company. Reprinted with permission.

humans. Even those arguing for the medical benefits of cloning human tissues in culture were careful to establish their decent credentials, in the most vigorous terms, by denouncing the very thought that adult humans might be cloned to make babies, like Dolly.

But is it so obviously repugnant that we shouldn't even think about it? Mightn't even you, in your heart of hearts, quite like to be cloned? As Charles Darwin said in another context, it is like confessing a murder, but I think I would. The motivation need have nothing to do with vanity, with thinking that the world would be a better place if there was another one of you living on after you are dead. I have no such illusions. My feeling is founded on pure curiosity. I know how I turned out, having been born in the 1940s, schooled in the 1950s, come of age in the 1960s, and so on. I find it a personally riveting thought that I could watch a small copy of myself, fifty years younger and wearing a baseball hat instead of a British Empire pith helmet, nurtured through the early decades of the twenty-first century. Mightn't it feel almost like turning back your personal clock fifty years? And mightn't it be wonderful to advise your junior copy on where you went wrong, and how to do it better? Isn't this, in (sometimes sadly) watered-down form, one of the motives that drives people to breed children in the ordinary way, by sexual reproduction?

Who would be cloned?

If I have succeeded in my aim, you may be feeling warmer towards the idea of human cloning than before. But now think about the following. Who is most likely to get themselves cloned? A nice person like you? Or someone with power and influence like Saddam Hussein? A hero we'd all like to see more of, like David Attenborough? Or someone who can pay, like Rupert Murdoch? Worse, the technology might not be limited to single copies of the cloned individual. The imagination presents the all-too plausible spectre of *multiple* clones, regiments of identical individuals marching by the thousand, in lockstep to a Brave New Millennium. Phalanxes of identical little Adolf Hitlers goose-stepping to the same genetic drum—here is a vision so horrifying as to overshadow any lingering curiosity we might have over the final solution to the "nature or nurture" problem (for multiple cloning, to switch to the positive again, would certainly provide an elegant approach to that ancient conundrum). Science can open our eyes in both directions, towards negative as well as positive possibilities. It cannot tell us which way to turn, but it can help us to see what lies along the alternative paths.

Human cloning already happens by accident.

Human cloning already happens by accident—not particularly often but often enough that we all know examples. Identical twins are true clones of each other, with the same genes. Hell's foundations don't quiver every time a pair of identical twins is born. Nobody has ever suggested that identical twins are zombies without individuality or personality. Of those who think anybody has a soul, none has ever suggested that identical twins lack one. So, the new discoveries announced from Edinburgh [i.e. Dolly] can't be *all* that radical in their moral and ethical implications.

Nevertheless, the possibility that adult humans might be cloned as babies has potential implications that society would do well to ponder before the reality catches up with us. Even if we could find a legal way of limiting the privilege to universally admired paragons, wouldn't a new Albert Einstein, say, suffer terrible psychological problems? Wouldn't he be teased at school, tormented by unreasonable expectations of genius? But he might turn out even better than the paragon. Old Einstein, however outstanding his genes, had an ordinary education and had to waste his time earning a living in the patent office. Young Einstein could be given an education to match his genes and an inside track to make the best use of his talents from the start.

Turning back to the objections, wouldn't the first cloned child feel a bit of a freak? It would have a birth mother who was no relation, an identical brother or sister who might be old enough to be a great grandparent, and genetic parents perhaps long dead. On the other hand, the stigma of uniqueness is not a new problem, and it is not beyond our wit to solve it. Something like it arose for the first in vitro fertilized babies, yet now they are no longer called "test tube babies" and we hardly know who is one and who is not.

Cloning is more natural than sex

Cloning is said to be unnatural. It is of more academic than ethical interest, but there is a sense in which, to an evolutionary biologist, cloning is more natural than the sexual alternative. I speak of the famous paradox of sex, often called the twofold cost of sex, the cost of meiosis, or the cost of producing sons. I'll explain this, but briefly because it is quite well known. The selfish gene theorem, which treats an animal as a machine programmed to maximize the survival of copies of its genes, has become a favored way of expressing modern Darwinism. The rationale . . . is that all animals are descended from an unbroken line of ancestors who succeeded in passing on those very genes. From this point of view, at least when naively interpreted, sex is paradoxical because a mutant female who spontaneously switched to clonal reproduction would immediately be twice as successful as her sexual rivals. She would produce female offspring, each of whom would bear all her genes, not just half of them. Her grandchildren and more remote descendants, too, would be females containing 100 percent of her genes rather than one quarter, one eighth, and so on.

Our hypothetical mutant must be female rather than male, for an interesting reason which fundamentally amounts to economics. We assume that the number of offspring reared is limited by the economic resources poured into them, and that two nurturing parents can therefore rear twice as many as one single parent. The option of going it alone without a sexual partner is not open to males because single males are not geared up to bear the economic costs of rearing a child. This is especially clear in mammals where males lack a uterus and mammary glands. Even at the level of gametes, and over the whole animal kingdom, there is a basic economic imbalance between large, nutritious eggs and small, swimming sperm. A sperm is well equipped to find an egg. It is not economically equipped to grow on its own. Unlike an egg, it does not have the option of dispensing with the other gamete.

The economic imbalance between the sexes can be redressed later in development, through the medium of paternal care. Many bird species are monogamous, with the male playing an approximately equal role in protecting and feeding the young. In such species the twofold cost of sex is at least substantially reduced. The hypothetical cloning female still exports her genes twice as efficiently to each child. But she has half as many children as her sexual rival, who benefits from the equal economic assistance of a male. The actual magnitude of the cost of sex will vary between twofold (where there is no paternal care) to zero (where the economic contribution of the father equals that of the mother, and the productivity in offspring of a couple is twice that of a single mother).

The onus is on objectors to produce arguments to the effect that cloning would harm somebody.

In most mammals paternal care is either nonexistent or too small to make much of a dent in the twofold cost of sex. Accordingly, from a Darwinian point of view, sex remains something of a paradox. It is, in a way, more "unnatural" than cloning. This piece of reasoning has been the starting point for an extensive theoretical literature with the more or less explicitly desperate aim of finding a benefit of sex sufficiently great to outweigh the twofold cost. A succession of books has tried, with no conspicuous success, to solve this riddle. The consensus has not moved greatly in the twenty years since Williams's 1975 publication, which began:

> This book is written from a conviction that the prevalence of sexual reproduction in higher plants and animals is inconsistent with current evolutionary theory . . . there is a kind of crisis at hand in evolutionary biology. . . .

and ended:

> I am sure that many readers have already concluded that I really do not understand the role of sex in either organic or biotic evolution. At least I can claim, on the basis of the conflicting views in the recent literature, the consolation of abundant company.

Nevertheless, outside the laboratory, asexual reproduction in mammals, as opposed to some lizards, fish, and various groups of invertebrates, has never been observed. It is quite possible that our ancestral lineage has not reproduced asexually for more than a billion years. There are good reasons for doubting that adult mammals will ever spontaneously clone themselves without artificial aid. So far removed from nature are the ingenious techniques of Dr. Wilmut and his colleagues; they can even make clones of *males* (by borrowing an ovum from a female and removing her own DNA from it). In the circumstances, notwithstanding Darwinian reasoning, ethicists might reasonably feel entitled to call human cloning unnatural.

Can cloning be proven wrong?

I think we must beware of a reflex and unthinking antipathy, or "yuk reaction" to everything "unnatural." Certainly cloning is unprecedented among mammals, and certainly if it were widely adopted it would interfere with the natural course of the evolutionary process. But we've been interfering with human evolution ever since we set up social and economic machinery to support individuals who could not otherwise afford to reproduce, and most people don't regard that as self-evidently bad, although it is surely unnatural. It is unnatural to read books, or travel faster than we can run, or scuba dive. As the old joke says, "If God had intended us to fly, he'd never have given us the railway." It's unnatural to wear clothes, yet the people most likely to be scandalized at the unnaturalness of human cloning may be the very people most outraged by (natural) nudity. For good or ill, human cloning would have an impact on society, but it is not clear that it would be any more momentous than the introduction of antibiotics, vaccination, or efficient agriculture, or than the abolition of slavery.

If I am asked for a positive argument in favor of human cloning, my immediate response is to question where the onus of proof lies. There are general arguments based on individual liberty against prohibiting anything that people want to do, unless there is good reason why they should not. Sometimes, when it is hard to peer into the future and see the consequences of doing something new, there is an argument from simple prudence in favor of doing nothing, at least until we know more. If such an argument had been deployed against X rays, whose dangers were appreciated later than their benefits, a number of deaths from radiation sickness might have been averted. But we'd also be deprived of one of medicine's most lifesaving diagnostic tools.

The fact that I hate something is not, in itself, sufficient justification for stopping others who wish to enjoy it.

Very often there are excellent reasons for opposing the "individual freedom" argument that people should be allowed to do whatever they want. A libertarian argument in favor of allowing people to play amplified music without restriction is easily countered on grounds of the nuisance and displeasure caused to others. Assuming that some people want to be cloned, the onus is on objectors to produce arguments to the effect that cloning would harm somebody, or some sentient being, or society or the planet at large. We have already seen some such arguments, for instance, that the young clone might feel embarrassed or overburdened by expectations. Notice that such arguments on behalf of the young clone must, in order to work, attribute to the young clone the sentiment, "I wish I had never been born because . . ." Such statements can be made, but they are hard to maintain, and the kind of people most likely to object to cloning are the very people least likely to favor the "I wish I didn't exist" style of argument when it is used in the abortion or the euthanasia debates. As for the harm that cloning might do to third parties, or to society at large, no doubt arguments can be mounted. But they must be strong enough to counter the general "freedom of the individual" presumption in favor of cloning. My suspicion is that it will prove hard to make the case that cloning does more harm to third parties than pop festivals, advertising hoardings, or mobile telephones in trains—to name three pet hates of my own. The fact that I hate something is not, in itself, sufficient justification for stopping others who wish to enjoy it. The onus is on the objectors to press a better objection. Personal prejudice, without supporting justification, is not enough.

Religious prejudices

A convention has grown up that prejudices based upon religion, as opposed to purely personal prejudices, are especially privileged, self-evidently exempt from the need for supporting argument. This is relevant to the present discussion, as I suspect that reflex antipathy to advances in reproductive technology is frequently, at bottom, religiously inspired. Of course people are entitled to their religious, or any other, convictions. But society should beware of assuming that when a conviction is religious this somehow entitles it to a special kind of respect, over and above the respect we should accord to personal prejudice of any other kind. This was brought home to me by media responses to Dolly.

> *Why has our society so meekly acquiesced in the idea that religious views have to be respected . . . without question?*

A news story like Dolly's is always followed by a flurry of energetic press activity. Newspaper columnists sound off, solemnly or facetiously, occasionally intelligently. Radio and television producers seize the telephone and round up panels to discuss and debate the moral and legal issues. Some of these panelists are experts on the science, as you would expect and as is right and proper. Others are distinguished scholars of moral or legal philosophy, which is equally appropriate. Both these categories of person have been invited to the studio in their own right, because of their specialized knowledge or their proven ability to think intelligently and express themselves clearly. The arguments that they have with each other are usually illuminating and rewarding.

But there is another category of obligatory guest. There is the inevitable "representative" of the so-and-so "community," and of course we mustn't forget the "voice" from the such-and-such "tradition." Not to mince words, the religious lobby. Lobbies in the plural, I should say, because all the religions (or "cultures" as we are nowadays asked to call them) have their point of view, and they all have to be represented lest their respective "communities" feel slighted. This has the incidental effect of multiplying the sheer number of people in the studio, with consequent consumption, if not waste, of time. It also, I believe, often has the effect of lowering the level of expertise and intelligence in the studio. This is only to be expected, given that these spokesmen are chosen not because of their own qualifications in the field, or because they can think, but simply because they represent a particular section of the community.

Out of good manners I shall not mention names, but during the admirable Dolly's week of fame I took part in broadcast or televised discussions of cloning with several religious leaders, and it was not edifying. One of the most eminent of these spokesmen, recently elevated to the House of Lords, got off to a flying start by refusing to shake hands with the women in the television studio, apparently for fear they might be menstruating or otherwise "unclean." They took the insult more graciously than I would have, and with the "respect" always bestowed on religious prejudice—but no other kind of prejudice. When the panel discussion got going, the woman in the chair, treating this bearded patriarch with great deference, asked him to spell out the harm that cloning might do, and he answered that atomic bombs were harmful. Yes indeed, no possibility of disagreement there. But wasn't the discussion supposed to be about cloning?

Since it was his choice to shift the discussion to atomic bombs, perhaps he knew more about physics than about biology? But no, having delivered himself of the daring falsehood that Einstein split the atom, the sage switched with confidence to geological history. He made the telling point that, since God labored six days and then rested on the seventh, scientists too ought to know when to call a halt. Now, either he really believed that the world was made in six days, in which case his ignorance alone disqualifies him from being taken seriously, or, as the chairwoman charitably suggested, he intended the point purely as an allegory—in which case it was a lousy allegory. Sometimes in life it is a good idea to stop, sometimes it is a good idea to go on. The trick is to decide *when* to stop. The allegory of God resting on the seventh day cannot, in itself tell us whether we have reached the right point to stop in some particular case. As allegory, the six-day creation story is empty. As history, it is false. So why bring it up?

A hollow argument

The representative of a rival religion on the same panel was frankly confused. He voiced the common fear that a human clone would lack individuality. It would not be a whole, separate human being but a mere soulless automaton. When I warned him that his words might be offensive to identical twins, he said that identical twins were a quite different case. Why? Because they occur naturally, rather than under artificial conditions. Once again, no disagreement about that. But weren't we talking about "individuality," and whether clones are "whole human beings" or soulless automata? How does the "naturalness" of their birth bear upon that question?

This religious spokesman seemed simply unable to grasp that there were two separate arguments going on: first, whether clones are autonomous individuals (in which case the analogy with identical twins is inescapable and his fear groundless); and second, whether there is something objectionable about artificial interference in the natural processes of reproduction (in which case other arguments should be deployed—and could have been—but weren't). I don't want to sound uncharitable, but I respectfully submit to the producers who put together these panels that merely being a spokesman for a particular "tradition," "culture" or "community" may not be enough. Isn't a certain minimal qualification in the IQ department desirable too?

On a different panel, this time for radio, yet another religious leader was similarly perplexed by identical twins. He too had "theological" grounds for fearing that a clone would not be a separate individual and would therefore lack "dignity." He was swiftly informed of the undisputed scientific fact that identical twins are clones of each other with the same genes, like Dolly except that Dolly's clone is older. Did he really mean to say that identical twins (and we all know some) lack the dignity of separate individuality? His reason for denying the relevance of the twin analogy was even odder than the previous one. Indeed it was transparently self-contradictory. He had great faith, he informed us, in the power of nurture over nature. Nurture is why identical twins are really different individuals. When you get to know a pair of twins, he concluded triumphantly, they even *look* a bit different.

Where morals and values are concerned, there are no certain answers to be found in books.

Er, quite so. And if a pair of clones were separated by fifty years, wouldn't their respective nurtures be even *more* different? Haven't you just shot yourself in your theological foot? He just didn't get it—but after all he hadn't been chosen for his ability to follow an argument.

Religious lobbies, spokesmen of "traditions" and "communities," enjoy privileged access not only to the media but also to influential committees of the great and the good, to governments and school boards. Their views are regularly sought, and heard with exaggerated "respect" by parliamentary committees. You can be sure that, if a royal commission were set up to advise on cloning policy, religious lobbies would be prominently represented. Religious spokesmen and spokeswomen enjoy an inside track to influence and power which others have to earn through their own ability or expertise. What is the justification for this? Maybe there is a good reason, and I'm ready to be persuaded by it. But I find it hard to imagine what it could be.

To put it brutally and more generally, why has our society so meekly acquiesced in the idea that religious views have to be respected automatically and without question? If I want you to respect my views on politics, science or art, I have to earn that respect by argument, reason, eloquence, relevant knowledge. I have to withstand counterarguments from you. But if I have a view that is part of my religion, critics must respectfully tiptoe away or brave the indignation of society at large. Why are religious opinions off limits in this way? Why do we have to respect them, simply because they are religious?

Which faith should be called upon?

It is also not clear how it is decided which of many mutually contradictory religions should be granted this unquestioned respect, this unearned influence. If we decide to invite a Christian spokesman into the television studio or the royal commission, should it be a Catholic or a Protestant, or do we have to have both to make it fair? (In Northern Ireland the difference is, after all, important enough to constitute a recognized motive for murder.) If we have a Jew and a Muslim, must we have both Orthodox and Reformed, both Shiite and Sunni? And then why not Moonies, Scientologists and Druids?

Society accepts that parents have an automatic right to bring their children up with particular religious opinions and can withdraw them from, say, biology classes that teach evolution. Yet we'd all be scandalized if children were withdrawn from art history classes that teach about artists not to their parents' taste. We meekly agree, if a student says, "Because of my religion I can't take my final examination on the day appointed, so no matter what the inconvenience, you'll have to set a special examination for me." It is not obvious why we treat such a demand with any more respect than, say, "Because of my basketball match (or because of my mother's birthday party, etc.) I can't take the examination on a particular day." Such favored treatment for religious opinion reaches its apogee in wartime. A highly intelligent and sincere individual who justifies his personal pacifism by deeply thought-out moral philosophic arguments finds it hard to achieve conscientious objector status. If only he had been born into a religion whose scriptures forbid fighting, he'd have needed no other arguments at all. It is the same unquestioned respect for religious leaders that causes society to beat a path to their door whenever an issue like cloning is in the air. Perhaps, instead, we should listen to those whose words themselves justify our heeding them.

Science cannot determine truth

Science, to repeat, cannot tell us what is right or wrong. You cannot find rules for living the good life, or rules for the good governance of society, written in the book of nature. But it doesn't follow from this that any other book, or any other discipline, can serve instead. There is a fallacious tendency to think that, because science cannot answer a particular kind of question, religion can. Where morals and values are concerned, there are no certain answers to be found in books. We have to grow up, decide what kind of society we want to live in and think through the difficult pragmatic problems of achieving it. If we have decided that a democratic, free society is what we want, it seems to follow that people's wishes should be obstructed only with good reason. In the case of human cloning, if some people want to do it, the onus is on those who would ban it to spell out what harm it would do, and to whom.

13

The Media and Politics Are Undermining Cloning Research

Robert A. Weinberg

Robert A. Weinberg, the winner of the 1997 National Medal of Science, is a member of the Whitehead Institute for Biomedical Research and a professor of biology at the Massachusetts Institute of Technology.

The media and political circus surrounding cloning is damaging serious scientific research. Therapeutic cloning, which has the potential for treating large numbers of human degenerative diseases, is being hampered in the media circus. In addition, religious and political opposition to therapeutic cloning threatens to stymie this promising reproductive technology. In the end, the wide use of therapeutic cloning will hinge not upon its inherent scientific value but upon its acceptance or rejection by the political establishment.

B iologists have been rather silent on the subject of human cloning. Some others would accuse us, as they have with predictable regularity in the recent past, of insensitivity to the societal consequences of our research. If not insensitivity, then moral obtuseness, and if not that, then arrogance—an accusation that can never be disproved.

The truth is that most of us have remained quiet for quite another reason. Most of us regard reproductive cloning—a procedure used to produce an entire new organism from one cell of an adult—as a technology riddled with problems. Why should we waste time agonizing about something that is far removed from practical utility, and may forever remain so?

The nature and magnitude of the problems were suggested by the Scottish scientist Ian Wilmut's initial report on the cloning of Dolly the sheep. Dolly represented one success among 277 attempts to produce a viable, healthy newborn. Most attempts at cloning other animal species—to date cloning has succeeded with sheep, mice, cattle, goats, cats, and pigs—have not fared much better.

Even the successes come with problems. The placentas of cloned fetuses are routinely two or three times larger than normal. The offspring are usually larger than normal as well. Several months after birth one group of cloned mice weighed 72 percent more than mice created through normal reproduction. In many species cloned fetuses must be delivered by cesarean section because of their size. This abnormality, the reasons for which no one understands, is so common that it now has its own name—Large Offspring Syndrome. Dolly (who was of normal size at birth) was briefly overweight in her young years and suffers from early-onset arthritis of unknown cause. Two recent reports indicate that cloned mice suffer early-onset obesity and early death.

Arguably the most successful reproductive-cloning experiment was reported last year by Advanced Cell Technology [ACT], a small biotech company in Worcester, Massachusetts. Working with cows, ACT produced 496 embryos by injecting nuclei from adult cells into eggs that had been stripped of their own nuclei. Implanting the embryos into the uteruses of cows led to 110 established pregnancies, thirty of which went to term. Five of the newborns died shortly after birth, and a sixth died several months later. The twenty-four surviving calves developed into cows that were healthy by all criteria examined. But most, if not all, had enlarged placentas, and as newborns some of them suffered from the respiratory distress typical of Large Offspring Syndrome.

The success rate of the procedure, roughly five percent, was much higher than the rates achieved with other mammalian species, and the experiment was considered a great success. Some of the cows have grown up, been artificially inseminated, and given birth to normal offspring. Whether they are affected by any of the symptoms associated with Large Offspring Syndrome later in life is not apparent from the published data. No matter: for $20,000 ACT will clone your favorite cow.

Imagine the application of this technology to human beings. Suppose that 100 adult nuclei are obtained, each of which is injected into a human egg whose own nucleus has been removed. Imagine then that only five of the 100 embryos thus created result in well-formed, viable newborns; the other ninety-five spontaneously abort at various stages of development or, if cloning experiments with mammals other than cows are any guide, yield grossly malformed babies. The five viable babies have a reasonable likelihood of suffering from Large Offspring Syndrome. How they will develop, physically and cognitively, is anyone's guess. It seems unlikely that even the richest and most egomaniacal among us, intent on recreating themselves exactly, will swarm to this technology.

System of peer review

Biological systems are extraordinarily complex, and there are myriad ways in which experiments can go awry or their results can be misinterpreted. Still, perhaps 95 percent of what biologists read in this year's research journals will be considered valid (if perhaps not very interesting) a century from now. Much of scientists' trust in the existing knowledge base derives from the system constructed over the past century to validate new research findings and the conclusions derived from them. Research journals impose quality controls to ensure that scientific observations and conclusions are solid and credible. They sift the scientific wheat from the chaff.

The system works like this: A biologist sends a manuscript describing his experiment to a journal. The editor of the journal recruits several experts, who remain anonymous to the researcher, to vet the manuscript. A month or two later the researcher receives a thumbs-up, a thumbs-down, or a request for revisions and more data. The system works reasonably well, which is why many of us invest large amounts of time in serving as the anonymous reviewers of one another's work. Without such rigorously imposed quality control, our subfields of research would rapidly descend into chaos, because no publicly announced result would carry the imprimatur of having been critiqued by experts.

The hype about cloning has made a shambles of [the peer-review] system, creating something of a circus.

We participate in the peer-review process not only to create a sound edifice of ideas and results for ourselves; we do it for the outside world as well—for all those who are unfamiliar with the arcane details of our field. Without the trial-by-fire of peer review, how can journalists and the public possibly know which discoveries are credible, which are nothing more than acts of self-promotion by ambitious researchers, and which smack of the delusional?

The hype about cloning has made a shambles of this system, creating something of a circus. Many of us have the queasy feeling that our carefully constructed world of science is under siege. The clowns—those who think that making money, lots of it, is more important than doing serious science—have invaded our sanctuary.

The cloning circus opened soon after Wilmut, a careful and well-respected scientist, reported his success with Dolly. First in the ring was Richard Seed, an elderly Chicago physicist, who in late 1997 announced his intention of cloning a human being within two years. Soon members of an international religious cult, the Raëlians (followers of Claude Vorilhon, a French-born mystic who says that he was given the name Raël by four-foot-high extraterrestrials, and who preaches that human beings were originally created by these aliens), revealed an even more grandiose vision of human cloning. To the Raëlians, biomedical science is a sacrament to be used for achieving immortality: their ultimate goal is to use cloning to create empty shells into which people's souls can be transferred. As a sideline, the Raëlian-affiliated company Clonaid hopes to offer its services to couples who would like to create a child through reproductive cloning, for $200,000 per child.

Neither Seed nor the Raëlians made any pretense of subjecting their plans to review by knowledgeable scientists; they went straight to the popular press. Still, this wasn't so bad. Few science journalists took them seriously (although they did oblige them with extensive coverage). Biologists were also unmoved. Wasn't it obvious that Seed and the Raëlians were unqualified to undertake even the beginnings of the series of technical steps required for reproductive cloning? Why dignify them with a response?

Would-be cloners

The next wave of would-be cloners likewise went straight to the mainstream press—but they were not so easily dismissed. In March of 2001, at a widely covered press conference in Rome, an Italian and a U.S. physician announced plans to undertake human reproductive cloning outside the United States. The Italian member of the team was Severino Antinori, a gynecologist notorious for having used donor eggs and *in vitro* fertilization to make a sixty-two-year-old woman pregnant in 1994. Now he was moving on. Why, he asked, did the desires of infertile couples (he claimed to have 600 on a waiting list) not outweigh the concerns about human cloning? He repeatedly shouted down reporters and visiting researchers who had the temerity to voice questions about the biological and ethical problems associated with reproductive cloning.

The American member of the team was Panayiotis Zavos, a reproductive physiologist and an *in vitro* fertilization expert at the Andrology Institute of America, in Lexington, Kentucky. "The genie is out of the bottle," he told reporters. "Dolly is here, and we are next." Antinori and Zavos announced their intention of starting a human cloning project in an undisclosed Mediterranean country. Next up was Avi Ben-Abraham, an Israeli-American biotechnologist with thwarted political ambitions (he ran unsuccessfully for the Knesset) and no reputable scientific credentials, who attempted to attach himself to the project. Ben-Abraham hinted that the work would be done either in Israel or in an Arab country, because "the climate is more [receptive to human cloning research] within Judaism and Islam." He told the German magazine *Der Spiegel*, "We were all created by the Almighty, but now we will become the creators."

Therapeutic cloning has the potential to revolutionize the treatment of a number of currently untreatable degenerative diseases.

Both Antinori and Zavos glossed over the large gap between expertise with established infertility procedures and the technical skills required for reproductive cloning. Confronted with the prospect of high rates of aborted or malformed cloned embryos, they claimed to be able to weed out any defective embryos at an early stage of gestation. "We have a great deal of knowledge," Zavos announced to the press. "We can grade embryos. We can do genetic screening. We can do [genetic] quality control." This was possible, he said, because of highly sensitive diagnostic tests that can determine whether or not development is proceeding normally.

The fact is that no such tests exist; they have eluded even the most expert biologists in the field, and there is no hope that they will be devised anytime soon—if ever. No one knows how to determine with precision whether the repertoire of genes expressed at various stages of embryonic development is being "read" properly in each cell type within an embryo. Without such information, no one can know whether the developmental program is proceeding normally in the womb. (The prenatal tests currently done for Down syndrome and several other genetic disorders can detect only a few of the thousands of things that can go wrong during embryonic development.)

Rudolf Jaenisch, a colleague of mine with extensive experience in mouse reproductive cloning, was sufficiently exercised to say to a reporter at the *Chicago Tribune*, "[Zavos and Antinori] will produce clones, and most of these will die in utero . . . Those will be the lucky ones. Many of those that survive will have [obvious or more subtle] abnormalities." The rest of us biologists remained quiet. To us, Antinori, Zavos, and Ben-Abraham were so clearly inept that comment seemed gratuitous. In this instance we have, as on other occasions, misjudged the situation: many people seem to take these three and their plans very seriously indeed. And, in fact, this past April, Antinori claimed, somewhat dubiously, that a woman under his care was eight weeks pregnant with a cloned embryo.

Therapeutic cloning

In the meantime, the biotechnology industry, led by ACT, has been moving ahead aggressively with human cloning, but of a different sort. The young companies in this sector have sensed, probably correctly, the enormous potential of therapeutic (rather than reproductive) cloning as a strategy for treating a host of common human degenerative diseases.

The initial steps of therapeutic cloning are identical to those of reproductive cloning: cells are prepared from an adult tissue, their nuclei are extracted, and each nucleus is introduced into a human egg, which is allowed to develop. However, in therapeutic cloning embryonic development is halted at a very early stage—when the embryo is a blastocyst, consisting of perhaps 150 cells—and the inner cells are harvested and cultured. These cells, often termed embryonic stem cells, are still very primitive and thus have retained the ability to develop into any type of cell in the body (except those of the placenta).

Mouse and human embryonic stem cells can be propagated in a petri dish and induced to form precursors of blood-forming cells, or of the insulin-producing cells of the pancreas, or of cardiac muscle or nerve tissue. These precursor cells (tissue-specific stem cells) might then be introduced into a tissue that has grown weak from the loss of too many of its differentiated worker cells. When the ranks of the workers are replenished, the course of disease may be dramatically reversed. At least, that is the current theory. In 2002 one version of the technique has been successfully applied to mice.

Therapeutic cloning has the potential to revolutionize the treatment of a number of currently untreatable degenerative diseases, but it is only a potential. Considerable research will be required to determine the technology's possibilities and limitations for treating human patients.

Some worry that therapeutic-cloning research will never get off the ground in this country. Its proponents—and there are many among the community of biomedical researchers—fear that the two very different kinds of cloning, therapeutic and reproductive, have merged in the public's mind. Three leaders of the community wrote a broadside early this year in *Science*, titled "Please Don't Call It Cloning!" Call therapeutic cloning anything else—call it "nuclear transplantation," or "stem cell research." The scientific community has finally awakened to the damage that the clowns have done.

Government reaction

This is where the newest acts of the circus begin. President George W. Bush and many pro-life activists are in one ring. A number of disease-specific advocacy groups that view therapeutic cloning as the only real prospect for treating long-resistant maladies are in another. In a third ring are several biotech companies that are flogging their wares, often in ways that make many biologists shudder.

Yielding to pressure from religious conservatives, Bush announced [in August 2001] that no new human embryonic stem cells could be produced from early human embryos that had been created during the course of research sponsored by the federal government; any research on the potential applications of human embryonic stem cells, he said, would have to be conducted with the existing repertoire of sixty-odd lines. The number of available, usable cell lines actually appears to be closer to a dozen or two. And like all biological reagents, these cells tend to deteriorate with time in culture; new ones will have to be derived if research is to continue. What if experiments with the existing embryonic-stem-cell lines show enormous promise? Such an outcome would produce an almost irresistible pressure to move ahead with the derivation of new embryonic stem cells and to rapidly expand this avenue of research.

For many biotech companies the peer-review process conducted by scientific journals is simply an inconvenient, time-wasting impediment.

How will we learn whether human embryonic stem cells are truly useful for new types of therapy? This question brings us directly to another pitfall: much of the research on human embryonic stem cells is already being conducted by biotech companies, rather than in universities. Bush's edict will only exacerbate this situation. (In the 1970s a federal decision effectively banning government funding of *in vitro* fertilization had a similar effect, driving such research into private clinics.)

Evaluating the science coming from the labs of the biotech industry is often tricky. Those who run these companies are generally motivated more by a need to please stock analysts and venture capitalists than to convince scientific peers. For many biotech companies the peer-review process conducted by scientific journals is simply an inconvenient, time-wasting impediment. So some of the companies routinely bypass peer review and go straight to the mainstream press. Science journalists, always eager for scoops, don't necessarily feel compelled to consult experts about the credibility of industry press releases. And when experts are consulted about the contents of a press release, they are often hampered by spotty descriptions of the claimed breakthrough and thus limited to mumbling platitudes.

ACT, the company that conducted the successful cow-cloning experiment and has now taken the lead in researching human therapeutic cloning, has danced back and forth between publishing in respectable peer-reviewed journals and going directly to the popular press—and recently tried to find a middle ground. . . . In the fall of 2001, with vast ambitions, ACT reported that it had conducted the first successful human-cloning experiment. In truth, however, embryonic development went only as far as six cells—far short of the 150-cell blastocyst that represents the first essential step of therapeutic cloning. Wishing to cloak its work in scientific respectability, ACT reported these results in a fledgling electronic research journal named *e-biomed: The Journal of Regenerative Medicine*. Perhaps ACT felt especially welcome in a journal that, according to its editor in chief, William A. Haseltine, a widely known biotech tycoon, "is prepared to publish work of a more preliminary nature." It may also have been encouraged by Haseltine's stance toward cloning, as revealed in his remarks when the journal was founded. "As we understand the body's repair process at the genetic level, we will be able to advance the goal of maintaining our bodies in normal function, perhaps perpetually," he said.

Electronic publishing is still in its infancy, and the publication of ACT's research report will do little to enhance its reputation. By the usual standards of scientific achievement, the experiments ACT published would be considered abject failures. Knowledgeable readers of the report were unable to tell whether the clump of six cells represented the beginning of a human embryo or simply an unformed aggregate of dying cells.

One prominent member of the *e-biomed* editorial board, a specialist in the type of embryology used in cloning, asked Haseltine how the ACT manuscript had been vetted before its publication. Haseltine assured his board member that the paper had been seen by two competent reviewers, but he refused to provide more details. The board member promptly resigned. Two others on the editorial board, also respected embryologists, soon followed suit. (Among the scientists left on the board are two representatives of ACT—indeed, both were authors of the paper.) Mary Ann Liebert, the publisher of the journal, interpreted this exodus as a sign that "clearly some noses were out of joint." The entire publication process subverted the potentially adversarial but necessary dynamic between journal-based peer review and the research scientist.

Adult stem cells

No one yet knows precisely how to make therapeutic cloning work, or which of its many claimed potential applications will pan out and which will not. And an obstacle other than experimental problems confronts those pushing therapeutic cloning. In the wake of the cloning revolution a second revolution has taken place—quieter but no less consequential. It, too, concerns tissue-specific stem cells—but ones found in the tissues of adults. These adult stem cells may one day prove to be at least as useful as those generated by therapeutic cloning.

Many of our tissues are continually jettisoning old, worn-out cells and replacing them with freshly minted ones. The process depends on a cadre of stem cells residing in each type of tissue and specific to that type of tissue. When an adult stem cell divides, one of its two daughters becomes a precursor of a specialized worker cell, able to help replenish the pool of worker cells that may have been damaged through injury or long-term use. The other remains a stem cell like its mother, thus ensuring that the population of stem cells in the tissue is never depleted.

Until two years ago the dogma among biologists was that stem cells in the bone marrow spawned only blood, those in the liver spawned only hepatocytes, and those in the brain spawned only neurons—in other words, each of our tissues had only its own cadre of stem cells for upkeep. Once again we appear to have been wrong. There is mounting evidence that the body contains some rather unspecialized stem cells, which wander around ready to help many sorts of tissue regenerate their worker cells.

In the end, politics will settle the debate in this country about whether human therapeutic cloning is allowed to proceed.

Whether these newly discovered, multi-talented adult stem cells present a viable alternative to therapeutic cloning remains to be proved. Many of the claims about their capabilities have yet to be subjected to rigorous testing. Perhaps not surprisingly, some of these claims have also reached the public without careful vetting by peers. Senator Sam Brownback, of Kansas, an ardent foe of all kinds of cloning, has based much of his case in favor of adult stem cells (and against therapeutic cloning) on these essentially unsubstantiated scientific claims. Adult stem cells provide a convenient escape hatch for Brownback. Their use placates religious conservatives, who are against all cloning, while throwing a bone to groups lobbying for new stem-cell-based therapies to treat degenerative diseases.

Brownback would have biologists shut down therapeutic-cloning research and focus their energies exclusively on adult stem-cell research. But no one can know at present which of those two strategies is more likely to work. It will take a decade or more to find out. Many biologists are understandably reluctant to set aside therapeutic-cloning research in the meantime; they argue that the two technologies should be explored simultaneously.

Precisely this issue was debated recently by advisory committees in the United States and Germany. The U.S. committee was convened by Bruce Alberts, the president of the National Academy of Sciences and a highly accomplished cell biologist and scientific educator. Quite naturally, it included a number of experts who are actively involved in exploring the advantages and disadvantages of stem-cell therapies. The committee, which announced its findings in January, concluded that therapeutic cloning should be explored in parallel with alternative strategies.

For their trouble, the scientists were accused of financial self-interest by Steven Milloy of Fox News, who said, "Enron and Arthur Andersen have nothing over the National Academy of Sciences when it comes to deceiving the public . . . Enter Bruce Alberts, the Wizard of Oz-like president of the NAS . . . On his own initiative, Alberts put together a special panel, stacked with embryonic-stem-cell research proponents and researchers already on the taxpayer dole . . . Breast-feeding off taxpayers is as natural to the NAS panel members as breathing."

The German committee, which reached a similar conclusion, was assembled by Ernst-Ludwig Winnacker, the head of his country's national science foundation. Winnacker and his colleagues were labeled "cannibals" by the Cardinal of Cologne. Remarks like the ones from Steven Milloy and the cardinal seem calculated to make public service at the interface between science and society as unappealing as possible.

President Bush, apparently anticipating the NAS panel's conclusion, has appointed an advisory committee all but guaranteed to produce a report much more to his liking. Its chairman, Leon Kass, has gone on record as being against all forms of cloning. (Earlier in his career Kass helped to launch an attack on *in vitro* fertilization.)

Meanwhile, a coalition of a hundred people and organizations recently sent a letter to Congress expressing their opposition to therapeutic cloning—among them Friends of the Earth, Greenpeace, the Sierra Club, the head of the National Latina Health Organization, and the perennial naysayer Jeremy Rifkin. "The problem with therapeutic cloning," Rifkin has said, "is that it introduces commercial eugenics from the get-go." Powerful words indeed. Few of those galvanized by Rifkin would know that therapeutic cloning has nothing whatsoever to do with eugenics.

Politics to settle the debate

Usually progress in biology is held back by experimental difficulties, inadequate instruments, poorly planned research protocols, inadequate funding, or plain sloppiness. But in this case the future of research may have little connection with these factors or with the scientific pros and cons being debated earnestly by members of the research community. The other, more public debates will surely be the decisive ones.

The clashes about human therapeutic cloning that have taken place in the media and in Congress are invariably built around weighty moral and ethical principles. But none of us needs a degree in bioethics to find the bottom line in the arguments. They all ultimately converge on a single question: When does human life begin? Some say it is when sperm and egg meet, others when the embryo implants in the womb, others when the fetus quickens, and yet others when the fetus can survive outside the womb. This is a question that we scientists are neither more nor less equipped to decide than the average man or woman in the street, than a senator from Kansas or a cardinal in Cologne. (Because Dolly and the other cloned animals show that a complete embryo can be produced from a single adult cell, some biologists have proposed, tongue in cheek, that a human life exists in each one of our cells.) Take your pick of the possible answers and erect your own moral scaffolding above your choice.

In the end, politics will settle the debate in this country about whether human therapeutic cloning is allowed to proceed. If the decision is yes, then we will continue to lead the world in a crucial, cutting-edge area of biomedical research. If it is no, U.S. biologists will need to undertake hegiras to laboratories in Australia, Japan, Israel, and certain countries in Europe—an outcome that would leave American science greatly diminished.

Organizations to Contact

The editors have compiled the following list of organizations concerned with the issues debated in this book. The descriptions are derived from materials provided by the organizations. All have publications or information available for interested readers. The list was compiled on the date of publication of the present volume; names, addresses, phone and fax numbers, and e-mail and Internet addresses may change. Be aware that many organizations take several weeks or longer to respond to inquiries, so allow as much time as possible.

American Association for Laboratory Animal Science (AALAS)
70 Timber Creek, Suite 5, Cordova, TN 38018-4233
(901) 754-8620 • fax: (901) 753-0046
e-mail: info@aalas.org • website: www.aalas.org
The AALAS is concerned with the production, care, and study of laboratory animals. The organization provides a medium for the exchange of scientific information on all phases of laboratory animal care and use through its educational activities and certification programs. The association publishes two bimonthlies, the newsletter *AALAS Bulletin* and the journal *Laboratory Animal Science*.

American Civil Liberties Union (ACLU)
125 Broad St., New York, NY 10004-2400
(212) 549-2500 • (800) 775-ACLU (2258)
e-mail: aclu@aclu.org • website: www.aclu.org
The ACLU champions the civil rights provided by the U.S. Constitution. Its members are becoming increasingly concerned that genetic testing may lead to genetic discrimination in the workplace—the refusal to hire or the termination of employees who are at risk for developing genetic conditions. The ACLU publishes a variety of handbooks, pamphlets, reports, and newsletters, including the quarterly *Civil Liberties* and the monthly *Civil Liberties Alert*.

American Life League (ALL)
PO Box 1350, Stafford, VA 22555
(703) 659-4171 • fax: (703) 659-2586
e-mail: sysop@aol.org
ALL is an educational pro-life organization that opposes abortion, artificial contraception, reproductive technologies, and fetal experimentation. It asserts that it is immoral to perform experiments on living human embryos and fetuses, whether inside or outside the mother's womb. ALL further contends that surrogate motherhood is contrary to moral law and violates the sanctity of marriage. Its publications include the policy statement *Creating a Pro-Life America*, the paper *What Is Norplant?*, and the booklet *Contraceptive Compromise: The Perfect Crime*.

American Medical Association (AMA)
515 N. State St., Chicago, IL 60610
(312) 464-5000
website: www.ama-assn.org

The AMA is the largest and most prestigious professional association for medical doctors. It helps set standards for medical education and practices and is a powerful lobby in Washington for physicians' interests. The association publishes monthly journals for many medical fields, including the *Archives of Surgery*, as well as the weekly *JAMA*.

American Society of Human Genetics (ASHG)
9650 Rockville Pike, Bethesda, MD 20814-3998
(301) 564-5375 • fax: (301) 530-7079
website: www.ashg.org

The ASHG is a professional society of physicians, researchers, genetic counselors, and others interested in human genetics. Committees within the organization deal with issues concerning the Human Genome Project, human genetics education, public policy, and social issues. The ASHG publishes the monthly *American Journal of Human Genetics*.

American Society of Law, Medicine, and Ethics (ASLME)
765 Commonwealth Ave., Suite 1634, Boston, MA 02215
(617) 262-4990 • fax: (617) 437-7596
website: www.aslme.org

The society's members include physicians, attorneys, health care administrators, and others interested in the relationship between law, medicine, and ethics. It takes no positions but acts as a forum for discussion of issues such as genetic engineering. The organization has an information clearinghouse and a library. It publishes the quarterlies *American Journal of Law* and *Journal of Law, Medicine, and Ethics*; the periodic *ASLME Briefings*; and books.

BC Biotechnology Alliance (BCBA)
1122 Mainland St., #450, Vancouver, BC V6B 5L1, Canada
(604) 689-5602 • fax: (604) 689-5603
website: www.biotech.pc.ca/bcba/

The BCBA is an association for producers and users of biotechnology. The alliance works to increase public awareness and understanding of biotechnology, including the awareness of its potential contributions to society. The alliance's publications include the bimonthly newsletter *Biofax* and the annual *Directory of BC Biotechnology Capabilities*.

Biotechnology Industry Organization (BIO)
1625 K St. NW, #1100, Washington, DC 20006
(202) 857-0244 • fax: (202) 857-0237
website: www.bio.org

BIO is composed of companies engaged in industrial biotechnology. It monitors government actions that affect biotechnology and promotes increased public understanding of biotechnology through its educational activities and workshops. Its publications include the bimonthly newsletter *BIO Bulletin*, the periodic *BIO News*, and the book *Biotech for All*.

Center for Biomedical Ethics
PO Box 33 UMHC, Minneapolis, MN 55455
(612) 625-4917

The center seeks to advance and disseminate knowledge concerning ethical issues in health care and the life sciences. It conducts original research, offers educational programs, fosters public discussion and debate, and assists in the formulation of public policy. The center publishes a quarterly newsletter and reading packets on specific topics, including fetal tissue research.

Council for Responsible Genetics
5 Upland Rd., Suite 3, Cambridge, MA 02140
(617) 868-0870 • fax: (617) 864-5164
website: www.fbresearch.org

The council is a national organization of scientists, health professionals, trade unionists, women's health activists, and others who work to ensure that biotechnology is developed safely and in the public interest. The council publishes the bimonthly newsletter *GeneWatch* and position papers on the Human Genome Project, genetic discrimination, germ-line modifications, and DNA-based identification systems.

Foundation for Biomedical Research
818 Connecticut Ave. NW, Washington, DC 20006
(202) 457-0654

The foundation supports humane animal research and serves to inform and educate the public about the necessity and importance of laboratory animals in biomedical research and testing. It publishes a bimonthly newsletter, videos, films, and numerous background papers, including *The Use of Animals in Biomedical Research* and *Testing and Caring for Laboratory Animals*.

Foundation on Economic Trends
1130 17th St. NW, #630, Washington, DC 20036
(202) 466-2823 • fax: (202) 429-9602

The foundation examines the environmental, economic, and social consequences of genetic engineering. It believes society should use extreme caution when implementing genetic technologies to avoid endangering people, animals, and the environment. The foundation publishes the books *Biological Warfare: Deliberate Release of Microorganisms* and *Reproductive Technology* as well as articles and research reports.

Genetics Society of America
9650 Rockville Pike, Bethesda, MD 20814
(301) 571-1825 • fax: (301) 530-7079

The society promotes professional cooperation among persons working in genetics and related sciences. It publishes the monthly journal *Genetics*.

Hastings Center
255 Elm Rd., Briarcliff Manor, NY 10510
(914) 762-8500

Since its founding in 1969, the Hastings Center has played a pivotal role in exploring the medical, ethical, and social ramifications of biomedical advances. The center publishes books, papers, guidelines, and the bimonthly *Hastings Center Report*.

Health Resources and Services Administration
Dept. of Health and Human Services, Genetic Services
5600 Fishers Ln., Rockville, MD 20857
(301) 443-1080 • fax: (301) 443-4842
website: www.hrsa.gov

The administration provides funds to develop or enhance regional and state genetic screening, diagnostic, counseling, and follow-up programs. It also provides funds to develop community-based psychological and social services for adolescents with genetic disorders. It has many publications available through its educational programs, and it produces directories and bibliographies on human genetics.

Incurably Ill for Animal Research
PO Box 1873, Bridgeview, IL 60455
(708) 598-7787

This organization consists of people who have incurable diseases and are concerned that the use of animals in medical research will be stopped or severely limited by animal rights activists, thus delaying or preventing the development of new cures. It publishes the monthly *Bulletin* and a quarterly newsletter.

International Genetics Federation (IGF)
University of British Columbia, Dept. of Botany
6270 University Blvd., Vancouver, BC V6T 1Z4 CANADA
(604) 822-5629 • fax: (604) 822-9179

Through its international network of genetics societies, the IGF works to further the science of genetics. The federation provides information about genetics and offers referrals to local genetics societies.

Kennedy Institute of Ethics
Georgetown University
1437 37th St. NW, Washington, DC 20057
(202) 687-8099 • (800) 633-3849 • fax: (202) 687-6779
website: http://guweb.georgetown.edu/kennedy

The institute sponsors research on medical ethics, including ethical issues surrounding the use of recombinant DNA and human gene therapy. It supplies the National Library of Medicine with an online database on bioethics and publishes an annual bibliography in addition to reports and articles on specific issues concerning medical ethics.

March of Dimes Birth Defects Foundation
1901 L St. NW, #206, Washington, DC 20036
(202) 659-1800 • fax: (202) 296-2964

The March of Dimes is concerned with preventing and treating birth defects, including those caused by genetic abnormalities. It monitors legislation and regulations that affect health care and research, awards grants for research, and provides funding for treatment of birth defects. The organization offers information on a wide variety of genetic diseases and their treatments, and it publishes the quarterly newsletter *Genetics in Practice*.

National Association for Biomedical Research (NABR)
818 Connecticut Ave. NW, Suite 303, Washington, DC 20006
(202) 857-0540 • fax: (202) 659-1902
website: www.nabr.org

The NABR comprises universities, research institutes, professional societies, animal breeders and suppliers, and pharmaceutical companies that use animals for biomedical research and testing. The association also monitors and, if necessary, attempts to influence government legislation regarding the use of animals in research and testing. Its publications include the *NABR Update*, published biweekly, and the *NABR Alert*, published six to ten times a year.

National Institutes of Health (NIH)
Health and Human Services Dept., Human Genome Research
9000 Rockville Pike, Bethesda, MD 20892
(301) 402-0911 • fax: (301) 402-0837
website: www.nih.gov

The NIH plans, coordinates, and reviews the progress of the Human Genome Project and works to improve techniques for cloning, storing, and handling DNA. It offers a variety of information on the Human Genome Project.

People for the Ethical Treatment of Animals (PETA)
501 Front St., Norfolk, VA 23510
(757) 622-7382
website: www.peta-online.org

PETA is an educational and activist group that opposes all forms of animal exploitation. It conducts rallies and demonstrations to focus attention on animal experimentation, the fur fashion industry, and the killing of animals for human consumption—three issues it considers institutionalized cruelty. PETA hopes to educate the public about human chauvinist attitudes toward animals and about the conditions in slaughterhouses and research laboratories. It publishes reports on animal experimentation and animal farming and the quarterly newsletter *PETA's Animal Times*.

Society for the Study of Social Biology (SSSB)
c/o Jacci L. Rodgers
Oklahoma City University
Meinders School of Business, Oklahoma City, OK 73106
(405) 521-5824 • fax: (405) 225-4511
website: www.okcu.edu

The SSSB is an association of biological, behavioral, and social science scholars interested in the study of heredity and population. It promotes discussion, advancement, and sharing of knowledge about the biological and sociocultural forces affecting human population and their evolution. The society publishes the quarterly journal *Social Biology*.

Bibliography

Books

Lori B. Andrews — *The Clone Age: Adventures in the New World of Reproductive Technology.* New York: Henry Holt, 1999.

Michael C. Brannigan — *Ethical Issues in Human Cloning.* New York: Seven Bridges Press, 2001.

Terence A. Brown — *Gene Cloning: An Introduction.* New York: Chapman and Hall, 1995.

Justine Burley, ed. — *The Genetic Revolution and Human Rights.* Oxford: Oxford University Press, 1999.

Ronald Cole-Turner, ed. — *Beyond Cloning: Religion and the Remaking of Humanity.* Harrisburg, PA: Trinity Press International, 2001.

Ronald Cole-Turner, ed. — *Human Cloning: Religious Responses.* Louisville, KY: Westminster John Knox Press, 1997.

Karl Drlica — *Understanding DNA and Gene Cloning: A Guide for the Curious.* New York: Wiley, 1997.

William Dudley, ed. — *The Ethics of Human Cloning.* San Diego, CA: Greenhaven, 2001.

Leon R. Kass and James Q. Wilson — *The Ethics of Human Cloning.* Washington, DC: The AEI Press, 1998.

Gina Bari Kolata — *Clone: The Road to Dolly, and the Path Ahead.* New York: William Morrow and Company, 1998.

Lane P. Lester and James C. Hefley — *Human Cloning: Playing God or Scientific Progress?* Grand Rapids, MI: Fleming H. Revell, 1998.

Glenn McGee — *The Perfect Baby: Parenthood in the New World of Cloning and Genetics.* Lanham: Rowman & Littlefield, 2000.

Gregory E. Pence — *Who's Afraid of Human Cloning?* Oxford: Rowman & Littlefield, 1998.

Gregory E. Pence, ed. — *Flesh of My Flesh: The Ethics of Cloning Humans.* Lanham: Rowman & Littlefield, 1998.

M.L. Rantala and Arthur J. Milgram — *Cloning: For and Against.* Chicago: Open Court, 1999.

Melinda A. Roberts — *Child Versus Childmaker.* Oxford: Rowman and Littlefield, 1998.

Lee M. Silver — *Remaking Eden: Cloning and Beyond in a Brave New World.* New York: Avon Books, 1997.

Wesley J. Smith — *Culture of Death: The Assault on Medical Ethics in America.* San Francisco: Encounter Books, 2000.

Ian Wilmut, Keith Campbell, and Colin Tudge	*The Second Creation: Dolly and the Age of Biological Control.* New York: Farrar, Straus and Giroux, 2000.

Periodicals

Edward Barnes et al.	"Noah's New Ark," *Time,* January 8, 2001.
Shannon Brownlee	"Designer Babies: Human Cloning Is a Long Way Off, but Bioengineered Kids Are Already Here," *Washington Monthly,* March 2002.
Jose B. Cibelli et al.	"The First Human Cloned Embryo," *Scientific American,* January 2002.
Eric Cohen et al.	"Cloning, Stem Cells, and Beyond," *The Human Life Review,* Summer 2001.
Economist	"America's Next Ethical War; the Moral War over Genes," April 14, 2001.
Economist	"Storm in a Test Tube; Cloning," December 1, 2001.
Gia Fenoglio	"What Cloning Has Wrought," *National Journal,* August 4, 2001.
Ellen Wilson Fielding	"When Rights Collide," *The Human Life Review,* Fall 2001.
Joannie Fisher	"The First Clone," *U.S. News & World Report,* December 3, 2001.
Joannie Fisher et al.	"The Cell Wars Begin," *U.S. News & World Report,* December 10, 2001.
Cynthia Fox	"Why Stem Cells Will Transform Medicine," *Fortune,* June 11, 2001.
David R. Gergen	"Trouble in Paradise," *U.S. News & World Report,* August 20, 2001.
Christine Gorman	"Cloning: Humans May Have It Easier," *Time,* August 27, 2001.
Paul Lauritzen	"Broadening the Debate on Cloning and Stem Cell Research," *America,* February 4, 2002.
Brian Lavendel	"Jurassic Ark," *Animals,* Summer 2001.
David Longtin et al.	"Cloning Red Herrings: Why Concerns about Human-Animal Experiments Are Overblown," *Policy Review,* February 2002.
Naomi Lubick	"First Human Clone?" *Science World,* February 25, 2002.
Celeste McGovern	"Brave New World," *The Report Newsmagazine,* March 18, 2002.
Celeste McGovern	"In Our Own Image: If the World Accepts Human Cloning, What Follows Promises to Be Far from Pretty," *The Report Newsmagazine,* September 10, 2001.
Neil Munro	"An Interesting Disinterest in Cloning," *National Journal,* September 8, 2001.

Charles Murtaugh   "Shun Cloning: Scientists Must Speak Out,"
                          Commonweal, May 18, 2001.

The Nation   "Send in the Clones," October 8, 2001.

Kate Pollitt   "It's a Bird, It's a Plane, It's . . . Superclone?" *The Nation*,
                          July 23, 2001.

Ramesh Ponnuru   "Lapse of Reason: The Libertarians and Cloning," *Na-
                          tional Review*, February 11, 2002.

Thomas A. Shannon   "Human Cloning: A Success Story or a Tempest in a Petri
                          Dish?" *America*, February 18, 2002.

John Shea   "What's Wrong with Human Cloning," *Catholic Insight*,
                          April 2001.

Lee M. Silver   "What Are Clones?" *Nature*, July 5, 2001.

Peter Singer   "The Year of the Clone?" *Free Inquiry*, Summer 2001.

Melissa Stewart   "Cloning: Hit or Miss?" *Science World*, March 26, 2001.

Time   "Cloning: Where Do You Draw the Line?" August 13,
                          2001.

John Travis   "Dolly Was Lucky: Scientists Warn That Cloning Is Too
                          Dangerous for People," *Science News*, October 20, 2001.

Patricia J. Williams   "I a Child, and Thou a Lamb," *The Nation*, February 2,
                          1998.

Index